The Healthy Lawn Handbook

The Healthy Lawn Handbook

LANE L. WINWARD

The Lyons Press
Guilford, Connecticut
An imprint of The Globe Pequot Press

The Lyons Press is an imprint of The Globe Pequot Press.

Printed in Canada

Designed by Compset, Inc.

10 9 8 7 6 5 4 3 2 1

Library of Congress Cataloging in Publication Data
Winward, Lane L.
    The healthy lawn handbook / Lane L. Winward
        p.   cm.
    Includes index.
    ISBN 1-58574-243-0   ISBN 1-55821-148-9
    1. Lawns—Handbooks, manuals, etc. I. Title.
SB433.W49   1992
635.9'647—dc20   92—2902
                                                        CIP

Contents

Introduction

Why does grass grow everywhere but where you plant it? It grows on top of your sidewalk, in the cracks of driveways, and it tenaciously and cruelly invades and takes over all of your ornamental flowerbeds with no regard for the ruination of your endless efforts at horticultural perfection. Ahh, but where you want it to grow, in your vast acres of glorious green lawn, there are pits, dead spots, and ghastly patches of noxious and unsightly weeds!

This revised edition of *The Healthy Lawn Handbook* has been designed to provide quick, up-to-date, useful information that will assist you in caring for your lawn and solving these aforementioned dilemmas that have plagued humans since lawns were first planted.

Most people who own a home of their own have a lawn to take care of. The new information provided here can take much of the frustrating guesswork out of this task. You will discover how to raise your lawn to peak appearance and to maintain this appearance with the latest techniques, generating neighborly envy for miles around. Few people have the time to gain the years of hands-on experience necessary to maintain beautiful grass. This book is intended to solve that problem, and it does it quite well; even if as the author, I do say so myself.

CHAPTER 1

Why Have a Lawn Anyway?

Lush, parklike expanses of lawn appear to be everywhere, but they often seem unattainable when it comes to your own yard. It seems to take far too much precious water and toxic fertilizer to get a lawn to look just barely green. And then, you've got parasites that kill the grass and weeds that apparently benefit from all of your hard work much more than the ungrateful grass.

So why grow a lawn at all? Why not simply utilize the understated but most effective *concrete?* Or why not grow ground covers or simple flowers instead? The answer is that nothing else offers the benefits and versatility of a thick green carpet of grass.

Most plants used as ground cover cannot survive the rigorous foot traffic that grass endures so well. As for flowers, no strains have yet to be developed that are able to cover acres of land and lock the soil down as efficiently as grass.

Lawns beautify any location—be it home, office, or park. Grasses help prevent massive soil erosion around the globe. Unlike concrete, in unbearably hot weather grass will actually cool air near the earth's surface, acting as a super-efficient, natural air-conditioner. Lawns even reduce noise pollution by absorbing sound.

And of course, what would the millions of recreational parks be without the acres of soft verdant grass? Imagine trying to play baseball in a field of flowers or trailing vines of groundcover! Nothing serves as well as grass.

Throughout the United States, city ordinances require companies to place certain amounts of lawn and garden for every dictated amount of store front or parking area, in order to beautify and change the sterile look of closely packed commercial areas. I believe (and so do others or these ordinances wouldn't exist) that without growing things breaking up the burning acres of oil-soaked asphalt, without lawns in *particular*, we would be a dead and dying society.

CHAPTER
2

Varieties of Grass

A successful lawn is one that grows evenly with uniform color and texture throughout the entire surface. One of the secrets to achieving even and verdant growth is to plant varieties of grasses that are suitable not only to your climate, but also to the growing conditions in different areas of your property.

There are many varieties of grass. There are grasses that grow fast and some that grow slowly, grasses that have broad leaves and those that have fine leaves. Some of these grasses should be mowed short while others must be cut long. The following are some general lawn characteristics you should consider in planning your new lawn or to improve an old one that exhibits problems.

Shade grass is for landscaped lawns that have an abundance of trees and/or areas that are shaded by buildings and fences. This grass makes do with little sunlight and is adept at fighting off mold and moss. As your landscape matures and more shade covers your yard, it is of great benefit to scatter shade grass seed throughout your lawn so that it can take root as your sun grass begins to weaken and die.

Sun grass is for lawn surfaces that will be subjected to direct sunlight for extended periods of time throughout the year. This grass sends down deep roots to reach and hold moisture and has blades capable of retaining water for longer periods without withering. It is used in park-like expanses of unshaded lawn. A good rule of thumb is to plant sun grass in areas that get more than five hours of direct sun each day in the primary growth months.

Dry area grass thrives in climates that have little annual rainfall, limited access to artificial watering systems, and hard, un-irrigated soil. Nevada, New Mexico, and Arizona are great places to plant dry season grasses.

Wet area grass will grow in dirt that is constantly moist or flooded. This grass fights mold and fungus well and is good at quickly dispersing water through evaporation and natural synthesis. Many places in North and South Carolina as well as Florida benefit from the use of grasses of this strain.

It is by planting and growing the particular strain that is best suited for your grounds that a healthy, lush, lawn is maintained. Many people are not aware of these subtle differences in lawn varieties so they mistakenly plant a sun grass throughout a whole plot, not thinking ahead to the time when the shade trees in one corner of their lot have grown broad and tall with great shady branches, causing the grass there to become sparse and die. Or sometimes they do the reverse with a shade strain, removing a tree and expecting the lawn to continue to grow as it did.

Expert advice and thoughtful planting is invaluable in choosing *which* grass is used *where* on your property. Considerable thought should also be devoted to what other conditions a lawn will be subjected to in the future. Will your lawn need to be durable enough to stand up to dogs and children, or will it be only for decoration and display? It is important to consult with a lawn specialist and plant accordingly to attain the maximum efficiency and beauty of the grass on your property.

MAKEUP OF A GRASS PLANT

A lawn is actually a colony made up of many thousands of individual grass plants. These plants grow from the *crown,* which sprouts directly from the ground. When cutting a lawn, if the crown is not damaged your lawn will continue to grow with barely a halt. Underneath the crown is an underground network of roots. These roots take in water and nutrients, and they anchor the plant.

Reaching up from the crown is the *primary shoot.* This is the first stem that develops from a seeded grass plant. The primary shoot is made up of *blades, collar, sheath, nodes,* and *internodes.* A blade and sheath together make up a leaf. A band called the collar marks the spot where the blade and sheath come together.

Blades and sheaths come from rounded joints called nodes. The sections of stem between the nodes are called internodes. Blade shoots that grow out from the crown but are beside the primary shoot are called *tillers.* The presence of many tillers will make a lawn thick, lush, and full in appearance.

Bunch grasses, such as ryegrasses and tall fescues, grow in close, interwoven clumps that completely fill a lawn space. Creeping grasses spread by stems that reach out, twisting and turning for a distance from the original rooted stem. These stems are called *rhizomes* if they reach out below the

A grass plant, with its parts.

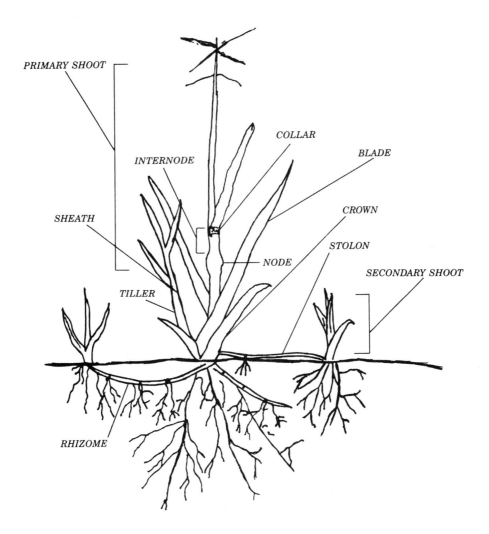

PRIMARY SHOOT

COLLAR

INTERNODE

BLADE

SHEATH

CROWN

STOLON

NODE

SECONDARY SHOOT

TILLER

RHIZOME

ground, and *stolons* if they reach out above the ground. Some grasses spread by rhizomes only and some spread by stolons only. Other grasses spread by both stolons and rhizomes.

SPECIFIC GRASS STRAINS

Grass strains are also categorized as either *warm season* or *cool season*. Cool season grasses grow very well in high elevations in the South and nearly all elevations in the North. These lawns grow profusely in the cool weather of the spring and fall, and slowly in the heat of summer. With adequate watering, these grasses will remain green all year round. Kentucky bluegrass, bent grass, ryegrass, and fescues are examples of cool season grasses.

Warm season grasses grow best in the southern parts of the United States. They grow actively in the warm summer months and then become dormant when cold weather strikes. These grasses turn brown in the cold season and will not do well in cold climates. Bermuda grass, Bahia grass, centipede grass, St. Augustine grass, and zoysia grass are common warm season grasses. Warm season grasses that will tolerate cold climates are Buffalo grass and Blue Grama.

In an effort to create more disease-resistant and hardier strains of grass, man has taken the basic strains and bred them together to create many different cultivated varieties. These *cultivars* are more resistant to insects and adverse growing conditions, and newer strains with better refinements and capabilities are created every year to replace the old cultivars. Thus, to solve a problem with an area that seems unable to support grass growth, perhaps a new cultivated variety can suit the needs of the difficult patch.

The following are just a few examples of different varieties of grasses and some of their characteristics.

Kentucky Bluegrass (cool season) is the most widely grown lawn grass. It is the principal variety in all good lawn mixtures. It is also frequently planted alone. Kentucky bluegrass thrives on most types of Western soils but is difficult to get started on heavily alkaline soils. Bluegrass also has many improved cultivars.

Kentucky bluegrass may suffer from summer heat and can be easily damaged by mowing too short. Fertilizer needs are medium to high and the cutting length should be from 1½ to 3 inches in summer.

Best areas for growth are the Sierra Nevada, the Rocky Mountains, the north-central and northeastern states, and the higher mountains of the upper South.

Cultivated varieties include Adelphi, Baron, Challenger, Eclipse, Fylking, Glade, Kenblue, Majestic, Newport, Parade, Rugby, Sydsport, Victa.

Creeping Red Fescue, Red Fescue (cool season) is often a component of bluegrass mixtures. Fescues do what many others cannot do—grow well in shade or dry soil. It has a high tolerance for ground acid. Fertilizer needs are low to medium and mowing heights are 1½ to 2½ inches.

Problems include susceptibility to summer diseases in hot, humid climates and slow recovery when damaged. The best regions for growth are those where the summers are not very hot, such as Oregon and other coastal north-west areas. They grow quite well in most of the Great Lakes region.

Some cultivars are Aurora, Banner, Cascade, C-26, Dawson, Fortress, Highlight, Jamestown, Reliant, Shadow.

Creeping Bent Grass (cool season) can grow in acid soil with poor drainage. This grass is used for golf-course putting greens, lawn bowling, and other similar types of lawns. Creeping bent must be cut quite low or it creates too much of a thatch layer. Similar to all bent grasses, creeping bent grass is susceptible to many diseases. It grows best in full sun with little shade.

Water needs are high for this grass and fertilizer needs are medium to high. Creeping bent grass grows best in the moist soils of the northern United States and Canada. Some cultivars are Penncross, Emerald, Seaside, Prominent, Penneagle.

Common Bermuda Grass (warm season) grows best in warm, humid climates. It stays green for most months of the year. Bermuda is easy to grow in most soils and will handle considerable traffic without damage. It has low maintenance requirements. Mow 1 to 1½ inches.

Problems with common Bermuda grass are browning in the fall until spring and very low shade tolerance. Fertilizer needs are medium to high and watering requirements are low. The best places to plant are the lower elevations of the Southwest, Maryland to Florida, Kansas, Oklahoma, and Texas.

The most prominent cultivar is Arizona Common.

Improved Bermuda Grass (warm season) has most of the same good points of common Bermuda grass but grows softer, thicker, and more finely textured. In most cases, a shorter dormant period is experienced.

More water is needed and more mowing than common Bermuda grass, and perhaps even more thatch control. It will generally not grow in shade. Fertilizer needs are medium to high and traffic tolerance is excellent. Mow ½ to 1 inch in height.

A few cultivars are Midway, Ormond, Santa Ana, Tifdwarf, Tifgreen.

St. Augustine Grass (warm season) will grow in salty soil and does well in shade. Augustine is also extremely fast growing and hardy. Water needs are high and fertilizer needs are medium to high. Cinch bugs can do considerable damage and this grass tends toward heavy thatch. St. Augustine is also prone to SAD virus (grass decline). Mowing height should be 2 to 3 inches.

Best areas to plant are southern California, Hawaii, mild areas in the Southwest, and Gulf Coast states.

Two cultivars are Bitter Blue and Floratam.

Bahia Grass (warm season) has low maintenance requirements and extensive root systems. These root systems are a great help in erosion control and require lower amounts of water.

Bahia has coarse blades, and, since it is fast growing, requires very frequent mowing to continue looking good. Fertilizer needs are medium. Mowing height should be 2 to 3 inches. The best regions in which to grow Bahia are the central coast of North Carolina to eastern Texas. It grows well in Florida also.

Cultivars are Argentine and Pensacola.

Zoysia Grass (warm season) forms a dense, fine-textured lawn that fights back against weeds and has good tolerance to heat and drought. It is also disease and insect resistant.

Zoysia is very slow to establish and will not grow where summers are short or cool. It will build too much thatch if over-fertilized or cut too long. Fertilizer needs are low to medium. Mowing height is 1 to 2 inches. It grows best in most southern climates.

Several cultivars are Meyer, El Toro, Belair, Emerald, and Manila.

Centipede Grass (warm season) is a good low-maintenance lawn. It lives well in poor soil and is hardy enough to crowd out weeds. It will require more mowing than most grasses.

Centipede is coarse textured, however, and is very light green and so does not appear as healthy as other strains. It is very sensitive to low temperatures and must be watched for thatch buildup. It has low fertilizer needs and should be mowed 1 to 2 inches. It has a very shallow root system.

Centipede grows best in the southern United States where there is high humidity. Cultivars are Centiseed, Oklawn, Centennial, Raleigh.

Grama Grass (warm season) is a non-decorative grass that is usually planted in rangeland or other never-watered situations. Grama is a native grass and can be difficult to find since there is little demand for its seeds. It has excellent heat tolerance and is good in arid and alkaline soils. It is not recommended for mowing areas. It has low fertilizer needs and grows best in the great plains, where it originates.

Turf-Type Perennial Ryegrass (cool season) has the trait of fast germination and establishment. It works well with many mixtures to create a fast growth for protection of finer strains that are slower growing. It has improved heat and cold tolerance along with resistance to heavy traffic.

Fertilizer needs are low to medium but water needs are high. Mowing height should be 1 to 2 inches. The best areas in which to grow it are coastal regions with mild winters and cool, moist summers.

Cultivars are All Star, Blazer, Citation II, Cowboy, Derby, Loretta, Manhattan II, Omega II, Palmer, Pennant, Penfine, Prelude, Premier, Regal.

Annual Ryegrass (cool season) is fast germinating and is often used as a temporary planting. It has poor heat and cold tolerance and does not mow well. Annual ryegrass gives protection for more permanent and hardy grasses to grow and establish but dies after one year, leaving these more permanent strains to flourish.

Fertilizer needs are low but watering needs are high. It should be mowed 1 to 2 inches.

Rough Bluegrass (cool season) grows well in wet, shady areas and so is a component of shady lawn mixtures. It has a shallow root system that will not tolerate dry weather. Water needs are high but fertilizer needs are low. It does not handle traffic well.

Mowing height should be 1 to 2 inches. The best areas for growth are the wet, shaded regions in the northern states. Cultivars are Sabre, Colt.

Hard Fescue and Chewings Fescue (cool season) have improved performance compared to other fine fescues because they have better resistance to heat, leaf spot, drought, red thread, and dollar spot. They grow well in the shade.

Hard fescue is slower to establish than other fine-textured lawns. Mowing height is 2 to 2½ inches and fertilizer needs are low. It grows best in regions where summer nighttime temperatures are moderate to fair.

Cultivars are the same as those of creeping red fescue.

At this point there are a few details that must be made clear. First, there are many more strains of grass that could be mentioned here. In fact, the list and specifications could go on for many, many pages. Also, for each of the strains, there are many more cultivated varieties than are mentioned. The strains and varieties that have been covered are those that are most prominent and widely used around the country. Second, though these different cultivars and strains are commonly used, they are difficult for the average property owner to find and purchase. Most individuals are lucky if they have a choice between cool season and warm season grass, especially if they are trying to go with sod as the method of planting. Therefore, in many instances, the knowledge of these many strains and varieties is extraneous knowledge at best.

But for those who are interested in extending their knowledge, for those who have the means and the intent to create a perfect lawn for their property, this knowledge can be very helpful. Each mentioned variety (and many more not mentioned) is available on the open market *somewhere*.

Most would have to be ordered and shipped to the recipient at what can be a considerable cost, but the results of ordering the perfect variety can be quite impressive.

For those individuals who do not have the means or the intent to go through the research and work to get these rare strains brought in, it is enough to try to get the correct sun grass and shade grass planted in the respective areas of their property. Where possible, it is also of great importance to insure that the correct warm season or cold season variety is chosen.

Research shows that the correct sun/shade and cold/warm decisions are the most important in creating a successful lawn.

CHAPTER 3

How to Plant a Lawn

When the road construction around my own house was finished at last, I rebuilt the sprinkler system and used the method of "seeding" to plant my lawn. As my house is on a prominent corner, for the month and a half it took for the lawn to completely take over, I fielded literally dozens of questions as to why I would choose such a slow method of grass replacement over the almost instant method of "sodding". Though most individuals know that I have planted hundreds of lawns in my career, a lot of heads were shaken in bewilderment that I would actually "go the long route." Then again, others probably thought that I was experimenting again just to see how things would work out.

When the grass had at last grown in noticeably thicker and greener than any lawn for blocks around, no one thought to congratulate me on choosing this method of planting over the other available options. Instead, everyone just wanted to know what fantastic strain of grass I had found that had grown with such great results. Week by week as my lawn grew thicker and greener, more and more people continued to ask the misguided question, *"What kind of grass did you plant?"*

Now, though I chose sun grass because that area of lawn is in the bright sunlight for nine hours a day in the summer, this beautiful lawn that I grew so quickly and perfectly was more a result of correct planting procedures than of the strain I chose. The fact is, even the most perfect strain, if planted wrong, will die.

As discussed in the previous chapter; for the best **long term** results, the right grass for different conditions should be chosen and applied whenever possible. It is in the beginning, however, that correct planting procedures should be applied in order for a lush and healthy growth pattern to form that will eventually keep diseases and pests from creating long term difficulties that can make you pull your hair out in frustration.

There are four types of planting procedures: *seeding, sodding, sprigging,* and *plugging.* Of the four, sodding is the most popular. With better techniques of growing, producing, and planting grass on large sod farms, sprigging and plugging have become seldom used procedures except where the use of warm season naturally growing grasses is a predominant factor. Some grasses (like hybrid Bermuda grass) do not produce viable seed and *must* be sprigged or plugged.

Seeding

Seeding is the cheapest method of planting grass. It is also the best method to use if you want to be sure of getting the highest quality and longest lasting successful lawn. There are two main methods of seeding: *drop seeding* or *hydro-seeding.*

The fastest and more expensive method of the two is *hydro-seeding.* Enough cannot be said about how well this method can work for you. The grass colonies come up strong and thick, and because of the hydration procedure, the germination time is very short. The only drawback of hydro-seeding is that the success of the application depends on the expertise and professionalism of the company that is performing the work. As in all cases of work for hire, it is important that you carefully check out the credentials of the company before letting them do your work.

As *drop seeding* is a method that property owners can apply for themselves, we will spend more time spelling out the best way to perform this type of grass planting operation. The seeds can be distributed by hand on most small sites, but for large areas you should use either a hand-held broadcast spreader or a rolling broadcast spreader. The best time to plant seed is in the early fall or early spring, though if water is easily available at any time during the heat of the day, summer works just fine as well.

When purchasing enough seed to cover an area, you will find statements by manufacturers on the seed packaging that will make claims such as, "Will cover 5,000 square feet." Since it is a law of nature that if you put down more seeds in a given area you will have a thicker lawn much more quickly, I make it a rule of thumb to figure that I will need three "5,000 square feet" bags to cover one actual 5,000 square foot area.

Sow half the seed by walking back and forth over the soil in an east to west track. Sow the other half by walking north to south. If at all possible, make sure that the seeds are laid down uniformly and evenly throughout the entire surface. Roll the soil lightly to compact the seeds gently down into the surface.

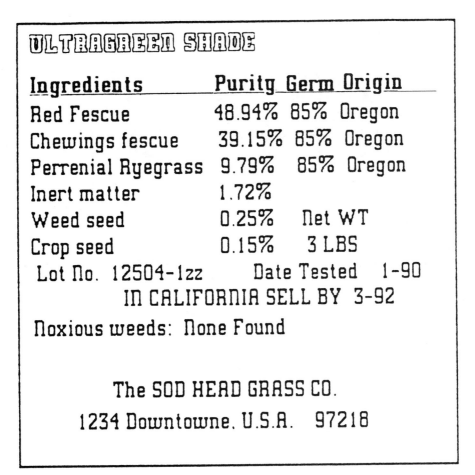

ULTRAGREEN SHADE

Ingredients	Purity	Germ	Origin
Red Fescue	48.94%	85%	Oregon
Chewings fescue	39.15%	85%	Oregon
Perrenial Ryegrass	9.79%	85%	Oregon
Inert matter	1.72%		
Weed seed	0.25%	Net WT	
Crop seed	0.15%	3 LBS	

Lot No. 12504-1zz   Date Tested   1-90
IN CALIFORNIA SELL BY 3-92

Noxious weeds: None Found

The SOD HEAD GRASS CO.
1234 Downtowne, U.S.A.   97218

This is a sample seed label that you will find on grass seed boxes, sacks, or containers. The portions of grass listed are only a sample. A good seed mixture is indicated by a low percentage of weed and crop seeds, an absence of noxious weeds and a high percentage of germination.

At this point it is important to cover the soil lightly with a layer of organic material. It is possible to use a light layer of straw or even a light layer of grass clippings from another lawn. The most successful and the most highly recommended covering is a quarter-inch of **peat moss**. In numerous experiments, grass seeds covered with a light layer of peat moss germinated three times as many sprouts as those covered with other materials. Peat moss also holds moisture around the seeds far longer than any other cover that is recommended for use.

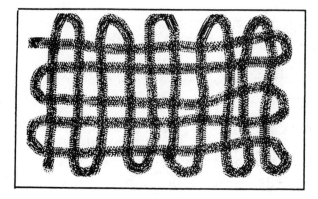

Sow seed and spread fertilizer in the same pattern. Walk back and forth over the area with half of the total amount and spread the other half by walking back and forth at right angles.

NOTE: Do not use steer manure of any kind for a cover. Not only can this natural product contain many noxious weed seeds, it can also prevent many of the seeds from growing due to fertilizer burn.

Once the seeds have been planted and covered, the most important part of the procedure begins, that of watering often and lightly. Over the years when I have been asked to explain how to seed a lawn, I have made it a practice to tell everyone I meet that I would not attempt it without having a decent sprinkler system. The reason for this is that when a seed gets water and sprouts a root, it takes only one hour of hot sunlight to bake the top inch of soil hard enough and dry enough to completely whither and kill this sprouted root. So, if you can only hand water once or twice a day, there is not much of a chance for successful germination of a large majority of the seeds. As soon as I plant a lawn, I immediately set the sprinkler system to water for six minutes, four times a day, dividing the four times into the number of hours that the sun will be shining each day.

Whether you use a sprinkler system or water by hand, it is not necessary to water for long periods of time. Not only will watering for long periods cause erosion and runoff, but it will do no good. The seed activity will all be in the first one inch of soil for the next month and a half after planting. Any water that is going down beyond this inch and a half will not help the lawn at all. As the first month and a half ends, I gradually cut back on my incidents of watering per day, and increase the length of watering time until I reach my optimum water schedule (See the chapter on watering).

NOTE: Seeding is the best method for one reason: The grass seeds that grow will be better acclimated to your particular area. Seeding is the "survival of the fittest" method. When you purchase sod (or even sprigs or plugs) the grass colonies you have bought may have been grown under conditions that are completely different from those of your lawn. For instance, to force sod to grow quickly at a sod farm, huge amounts of fertilizer may have been used. If this were the case with your sod, and you did not keep using enormous amounts of regularly applied fertilizer, your sod would soon become sickly and thin, perhaps even fading away entirely. The same sort of problem applies to how your purchased sod has been watered as it grew. If you do not maintain this same type of watering schedule, the lawn can become thin and yellow for quite some time until it acclimatizes itself, and even then, it may not do so to the point of lushness.

Seeded lawns never go through this acclimatization because you set the correct methods and schedules all by yourself from the very beginning.

Sodding

This is usually the fastest, easiest, and consequently the most expensive method of planting a lawn. Squares of soil already covered with grass are dug up (usually from vast sod farms) and placed directly on top of the soil of a lawn site. This method is most important to use on slopes that could quickly erode if planted another way. There is less preparation and a site is provided with a viable growing lawn almost instantly. This method provides, for all intents and purposes, an "Instant Lawn" that can be walked on and used (in a limited fashion at first) in only a week or so. The only drawback is that of the previously mentioned acclimatization factor. Many would consider the high cost a drawback also. In most cases you can hydro-seed a lawn for one third the cost of sodding, and you can drop seed a lawn for only one fifth of the cost of sodding.

Sprigging

This procedure involves the use of *sprigs;* small chunks or cuttings of grass. Sprigs are planted at regular intervals, depending on the variety of grass. As the sprigs grow, their low-lying stems creep along the ground and root in the soil, thus eventually filling in the entire lawn site. Sprigging is an extremely slow way to create a whole lawn in comparison to other techniques so most people do not utilize this method, (though the practice is still somewhat com-

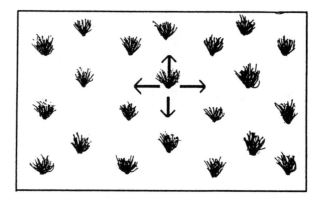

Sprigs are planted eight to ten inches apart and are copiously fertilized and watered. Sprig plantings are intended to spread in all directions and eventually fill in the entire planted area.

mon in some areas of the Southern states). Sprigs are usually made up of one of the *creeping* strains of grass.

Plugging

Plugs are made up of small squares or circles that are cut from sod and are planted 6 to 12 inches apart in much the same pattern as sprigging. Because the squares are thicker and larger than sprigs, the grass will fill in a bit faster. Though they need to be kept moist, plugs will not dry out as fast as sprigs, lasting a day or two longer in high heat conditions. Again, it must be stressed that the use of this method is very rare, and good results take a long time to achieve.

PLANTING PREPARATIONS

Much of the success in planting a lawn depends on how well the soil is prepared beforehand. Unlike a vegetable or flower garden, where the soil can be changed and built up each fall and spring, a lawn grows in the same soil year after year.

Although most nutrient deficiencies can be corrected after the lawn has been established, changing the soil texture under a growing lawn is difficult and quite expensive. The effort spent in preparing the soil beforehand will be rewarded by the health and beauty of your lawn for years to come.

This is true for seed lawns as well as sod lawns. Even though sod has a little soil already attached, soil preparation is still very important to long term success.

Plan Ahead

Remove the top six inches of soil. Put it off to one side and save it for respreading. Remove any debris—plaster, stones, and trash; do not bury it. Fill any trenches or depressions with soil and thoroughly settle with water. If a sprinkler system has been installed, it is a good idea to water for two solid weeks to settle possible depressions before moving on to planting.

Grade the Lawn

The grade should be sloped slightly—away from the house—to carry off surplus water. Avoid steep slopes; gentle and smooth slopes are prettier and easier to maintain. A 1- to 1½-foot drop in 10 linear feet is excellent. For steeper grades, ground covers other than grass might be used more efficiently. From long experience, I have found it quite hard (not to mention dangerous) to mow steeper grades. To my mind, different strains of Ivy or even growths of Vinca are better suited for growth on steep hills.

Stay away from abrupt changes in grade that result in burned or dried spots and mower-scalped crests. To keep lawn areas at minimum grade, use retaining walls of concrete or oiled wood.

Study Existing Soil

There are three principal types of soil: sand, clay, and loam. Sandy soil is made up of small rock particles. It drains easily but may lack humus—the required organic matter that is found in good soil. Clay soil is made up of very fine, dust-like particles of disintegrated rock. It holds tremendous quantities of water on the surface and frequently has poor drainage. In hot climates, clay can bake as hard as a rock and practically squeeze the life out of grass roots. Loamy soil is an easily crumbled mixture of different proportions of clay, sand, and organic plant matter. It is the ideal mixture for lawn growth.

If you have sandy or clay soil, there are many things you can do to change the physical characteristics of either one. Soil rebuilding with peat moss and commercial fertilizer is usually cheaper than excavating and refilling with new soil.

Fertilize Your Soil

The best way to improve soil is to mix in (with the garden tool of your choice) as much organic fertilizer as possible. Leaves and grass and compost are best. Peat moss creates an ideal seed bed.

Don't waste humus by mixing it too deep. Stay within the top four or five inches. If your soil is extremely gravelly or filled with clay, or if it is necessary to raise the grade, then you will need to bring in some topsoil. Be careful to get only the best quality. If your sprinkler system is not yet placed, do so before bringing in or finishing the spreading of the top soil layer.

Prepare the Seed Bed

After your grade has been established and your humus and fertilizer have been mixed into the soil, or following the spreading and improving of added topsoil, your area is ready for sodding or seeding.

If the previous steps have been done right this should be a simple job. Using a lawn rake, pull all high spots into the low spots until the surface is as smooth as possible. Rolling with a heavy roller at this stage will reveal any soft spots that would later sink and cause depressions.

To finish the lawn bed, remove all stones over an inch in diameter and, with a rake, powder the soil into a fine uniform texture by breaking up all clods and

The best way to even out a planting surface is to use a roller (usually filled with water for necessary weight) over the entire area to be planted.

smoothing the surface. Rocks just under the surface cause the grass to dry in spots during hot weather. A smooth seedbed of uniform texture absorbs water evenly, insuring uniform germination of all seeds and growth of the lawn that eventually forms. It also insures easier mowing.

Prevent Weed Growth

This step can be eliminated if your soil is not badly contaminated with weed seeds. Different quantities of weed seeds occur in all soils. The annual weeds will die after several cuttings and do not usually come back. There are certain chemicals, however, that when applied can make your lawn weed-free from the start. Some of these are mentioned in a later chapter. For the most current applications, brands, and amounts, contact your local nursery experts.

Select a Good Lawn Seed/Turf

This may well be the most important decision you will make regarding your new lawn. It will certainly have the most far-reaching influence on lawn beauty and on its later maintenance requirements.

As was mentioned in the previous chapter, there are grasses that grow fast and those that grow more slowly. There are grasses for damp areas, shade, and direct sunlight. Analyze your lawn and pick out the seed/turf that will grow best in each section.

Do not be afraid to have different varieties of grass in different areas of your yard. This is a necessary procedure for a successful lawn.

When Planting, Sow the Seed Correctly

Grass seed can be spread either by hand or by a seeder. With either method of spreading seed, use a crisscross pattern and avoid spotty coverage. In this procedure you spread half of the seed amount while walking north and south, and the other half while walking east and west.

Cover the seed by lightly raking over the surface, and then, if a roller is available, roll lightly to press the seed gently into the soil. A one-quarter-inch dressing of peat moss spread evenly over the surface will conserve moisture and ensure better, more even germination.

When Sodding, Lay the Sod Correctly

The ground should be deeply watered for a week before laying the sod. Lay the sod in a bricklayer's pattern, making sure that the slanted edges are matched to fit evenly. If the edges are matched correctly, grass on the sod square edges will not die. Use a sharp sod-cutting tool to make the sod fit around obstructions. Do not be afraid to cut the sod. Just ensure that the edges are well matched.

When the sod is laid, lightly roll the entire surface to ensure evenness.

Keep Traffic Off

It is important to keep traffic off a newly seeded or sodded lawn. If a fence is impractical, a humorous sign may help win cooperation. For example, you might write, "Your feet are killing me!"

A seeded lawn should have little or no traffic for at least a month. Sodded lawns should be protected for at least a week if not two.

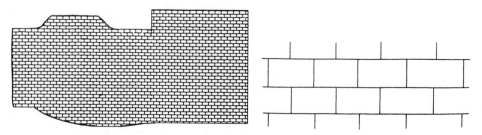

Good sod companies cut sod edges with these angles. This enables a good interlocking fit for sod placement.

For best growth between edges, sod is placed in a bricklayer's pattern. This pattern should continue throughout, even when the laying area is not an equal-sided shape.

Water Frequently

A lot of work and valuable sod or seed can be wasted and a lawn can be a complete failure if adequate water is not supplied frequently during the germination/rooting period.

Watering should be done slowly and lightly but must be frequent enough to avoid drying of the surface soil where the new tender roots and shoots are gaining a foothold. If you do not have a sprinkler system, early morning and mid-afternoon watering is best to keep the new grass and soil moist throughout the day.

Points to Remember

- Your first cutting should not occur until the seeded or sodded lawn has reached a fairly uniform length of three and one-half inches.
- Very small amounts of fertilizer applied weekly will ensure continued food for a new lawn.
- Use extreme caution with weed killers in the first year. Hand remove very troublesome weeds.

CHAPTER
4

Watering

PROCEDURES

In some highly humid climates, the practice of watering lawns is nearly unnecessary. Even during dry periods these lawns need only be watered a couple of times weekly. Daily watering may cause weeds, fungus, or weedy grasses to grow more rapidly than the lawn grass itself. To people in these climates we can only say "We salute you!" You are lucky people and the rest of us can only wish that we were as fortunate as you.

Those of us, however, who reside in the many climate zones that are *dry* and require considerable amounts of watering, can save much time and a lot of money on water bills by utilizing and adhering to a few simple rules and recommendations.

Water Depth

Water should be penetrating soil to a depth of 6 to 12 inches or more. Underneath trees water should soak down to a depth of 2 to 4 feet in order to ensure that tree roots continue feeding in their natural zone and out of competition with a lawn. This deep watering encourages food- and moisture-seeking grass roots to reach farther down. Deeper root systems mean thicker and more beautiful lawns.

It takes one inch of measured water to penetrate 6 to 12 inches in the average soil mix. To cover 1,000 square yards with one inch of water takes 624 gallons, or 83 cubic feet. WOW! The average sprinkler system will require twenty minutes of continuous spraying to attain this sort of coverage.

Yet, if a soil is sandy, water will pass through so quickly that lengthy watering does no good at all. Instead, decreased watering time and increased incidents per day will be called for.

Soil Timing

Timing will be different for various types of soil. You can figure that if sandy soil requires twenty minutes to soak one foot deep, loam would require thirty minutes. Under the same conditions clay would take about fifty minutes or more. It is important for clay soils not to be left dry for long periods because the hot sun can bake the clay soil almost rock hard.

Night Watering

It is best to water after or before the daylight hours because during a warm day more than 30 percent of the sprinkled water will evaporate before penetrating the soil (depending on the condition of the soil). If the day is very hot, an even higher percentage can just *melt* away and be absolutely useless to your lawn.

The cooler temperatures of nighttime or early morning allow water to soak through a soil and stay present for hours longer than during the heat of the day. This allows a lawn to drink for longer periods and to stockpile moisture against the coming heat. Very late evenings or extremely early mornings are best for watering. Quite often water pressure will also be much higher at this time because of less home use.

Heavy Sprinkling

If water is to be sprayed on an established lawn either by hand or with a system, it should never be sprinkled for only a short time. Daily light sprinkling fosters shallow rooting, fungus diseases, and the growth of crabgrass. The only exception to this rule is if your soil makeup is of a deep sand base. In this case, once enough water has been applied to soak the first two inches of sod base, the rest will just pass right through and do no good. With loamy and/or clay soils, however, the better method is to sprinkle (either by hand or system) for twenty to forty-five minutes in each location.

Slopes

If a large area of lawn with a long slope needs to be watered with several different lines or hand settings, the length of watering time should be shorter for the lawn at the bottom of the slope than the lawn at the top. The reason for this is that the water will continuously run downhill, causing the grass at the bottom to need less direct watering. This is an important detail to incorporate into your watering program because the flooded grass at the bottom of a hill is where many diseases take hold.

Flooding

If a lawn is being watered too much, puddles will form in depressions. This is an indication of poor drainage and is often where fungus, diseases, and undesirable creeping grasses can take hold. In these areas it is wise to cut back on water or to, wherever possible, create better drainage.

Remember:

- Not all dead brown spots are a result of not enough water. Many things such as chemicals, pests, and poor soil drainage, or too much soil drainage, can account for this.
- In climates with temperatures in the high nineties it can be necessary to water more than once a day.
- Good watering procedures consist of regular schedules, uniform coverage, and correct timing.

SPRINKLER SYSTEMS

After years of experience with thousands of lawns in more than five states, I have come to the conclusion that in most areas (especially the western states) there is no way to create and maintain a green and beautiful lawn without ensuring that water is spread regularly and evenly with the use of a good artificial watering source, otherwise known as a *sprinkler system*.

Certainly, it is a fact that grass grows perfectly well all by itself in the mountains, in the plains areas, and it is most certain to grow naturally and with amazing lushness in your gardens and sidewalks whenever you do not want it to. This naturally grown grass, however, is only a poor distant cousin to the genetically inbred grass that we expect to populate our property expanses with. The cultivated varieties of grass that we try to grow as lawns in the style of a flawless carpet really require the type of watering program that only a good sprinkler system can supply on a regular basis. The adding of water, in the right amounts and in the right places, is essential to lawn care in all but those few lucky climates.

Why Use a Sprinkler System Over Hand Watering?

In this wonderful age of easily found and cheaply purchased PVC piping, just about everyone can afford and has had installed (or is planning on installing) a good sprinkler system on their property. But still, in certain areas, I continue to run into people who question whether a system is worth having.

The first and foremost reason to install a system is ease of use. Even manual sprinkler systems can be turned on in a moment and left to run with no worry or checkup. There are no questions as to whether the sprinkler has been placed in the most advantageous position or whether it can be moved without soaking the person in charge. And of course, with even a moderately good electrical timer on their system, a person does not even have to worry about being in town to ensure that every blade and flower receives the correct and regular amount.

Other advantages include better coverage in less time, increased ability to follow correct watering procedures, and savings on water bills because of more economical use. Also, with better water management your ability to regulate fungus and control mold is greatly increased.

Why an Electrical System Over Manual?

With the great advances made in producing inexpensive electrical water timers, manual sprinkler systems are just about obsolete. But for those people who might be considering such an option, or for those who had a manual system put in long ago and are considering upgrading, a manual in-ground system only will work as well as an electrical one as long as the correct times and watering schedules discussed later in this chapter are adhered to.

But a manual system is **obviously** not nearly as time-saving and worry-free as an electrical system. You do have the small satisfaction of knowing that the sprinkler heads are completely covering your lawn, but *someone* must still be present to switch to each new line as the watering period is over, and *someone* must still be there to turn the system off when every section has been covered. And unless much effort is spent to ensure accurate time and amounts, the ability to regulate fungus and mold growth is lost.

SPRINKLER SYSTEM DETAILS

How Does a Sprinkler System Work?

Briefly explained, a heavy duty, underground, on/off ball valve is added as an extension to your underground water supply pipe. This on/off valve allows pressurized water to be supplied to a set of surface sprinkler valves during the growing seasons, and allows the same water supply to be cut off during the winter seasons.

The surface valves are always set to be in a shutoff mode until an electrical current is applied to a special solenoid on the surface valve. When the current is applied, the valve allows water to pass through to pipe lines with sprinkler heads attached. A timer supplies the electrical current that opens each surface valve at specific intervals and durations. This timer is connected to each valve, called a "Station," and is designed to cover a specific area of the lawn or garden. A correctly designed sprinkler system has enough stations to easily cover and even overlap coverage of the entire yard.

Electrical Timers

Simple electrical timers are equipped with internal workings that will rotate and set off each sprinkler line in the system once every twenty-four hours. Better timers will allow you to set the timer to go off only on certain days and not on others. Timers even better than these will provide the added capability of having certain lines activate more than once in a given twenty-four-hour cycle.

But the best timers, according to most reports, are digital ones that feature the following attributes:

- Accurate A.M., P.M. clock
- Ability to program from one to four watering periods in a twenty-four-hour span
- Ability to have some lines go off twice or more a day while other lines go off only once
- Ability to easily set individual running times for each station
- Easy access to manual turn-on for irregular occasions when extra running time might be required
- Easy access to manual turn-off for occasions of prolonged rainy weather.
- Battery backup in case of power failure
- Eight- to twelve-sprinkler-line capacity
- Two-week programming period

Metal pipe vs. PVC Pipe

As inexpensive timers have made manual watering a nearly obsolete practice, PVC piping has made the use of metal piping nearly non-existent. Certainly metal pipe is extremely difficult to break and to damage. Light freezing and expanding will not turn the metal piping brittle for many years. But today PVC (polyvinyl chloride) pipe is used almost exclusively for many reasons.

Plastic pipe does not fill up with mineral growth and rust. Installation of PVC is much simpler because there is no need to thread and join ends that must be cut. Plastic pipe is easily "primered," glued, and sealed against leaking. Also, individual pieces of plastic pipe can be cut to measure in seconds with very inexpensive tools. Not so with metal pipe!

To make plastic pipe perform to the highest standards a few simple steps should be followed.

1. Be sure that each line is buried between six and ten inches in depth. If a pipe is too close to the surface, it can be easily damaged. If it is buried too far, repairs and changes will be difficult.

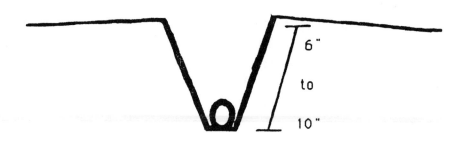

Sprinkler pipe should be buried six to ten inches deep to insure no damage from freezing or machinery.

2. For economical reasons, some companies or individuals may use thinner-gauge pipe throughout a sprinkler system. This is a **BAD** idea because over time, thinner pipe (⅛" or less) becomes brittle and can break even under normal everyday water pressure. Thinner gauge is also much more difficult—if not impossible at times—to repair.

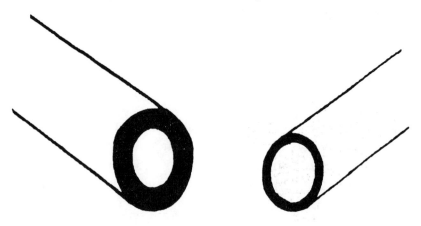

Always use thicker-gauge pipe. Thin gauge becomes brittle and is difficult to repair.

About Sprinkler Heads

The idea behind having a sprinkler system is to create an established pattern of spraying heads that completely and *thoroughly* covers all areas needing water. Following are descriptions of different sprinkler heads with a brief description of their characteristics.

Rainbird type. These heads are used to cover large areas because of their ability to spray long distances. School yards and parks utilize these heads. They spread water side to side at varying speeds to insure that water is flung in broken drops to the entire surface of the intended coverage area. These heads can spray straight and long, or a screw can be turned to break up the spray in portions that are not flung as far. Caution is advised when using rainbirds; coverage of all heads **must** be overlapped or dry spots can occur due to uneven watering.

Gear Drive watering. These heads spray like the above, but they move side to side more slowly, in theory to cover more evenly. They usually come in the "pop up" variety, and the best brands feature an excellent adjuster to break up the spray. Still, as with rainbirds, it is important to be sure that the area of coverage for each head is generously overlapped.

Orbit watering heads. These heads spray in a circular pattern either in full, half, or quarter circles. These heads provide excellent coverage if the placement is thought out correctly. There will be a problem with clogging if for any reason dirt is allowed in the line. They also must be carefully placed so that they are high enough to spray without obstruction by the growing grass blades, but low enough not to be chopped off by a lawn mower.

Pop-up Orbit heads. These heads are the same as the heads above except that when the water pressure is on, an extender rises. These heads can be set more easily lower down in the grass to avoid being run over by a mower because

Standard rainbird-type sprinkler heads are used to cover large areas. Their spray must overlap to insure total coverage.

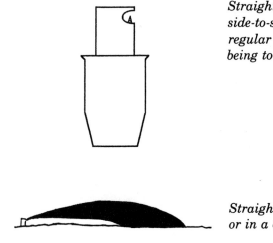

Straight rainbird heads move side-to-side much more slowly than regular rainbird heads, the purpose being to cover more evenly.

Straight rainbirds move side to side or in a complete circle.

the extender will rise up to the position necessary for correct coverage when water pressure is applied.

Inside of the more expensive of these heads, a spring is placed on the extender to bring it back into the closed position when the water is shut off. Cheaper heads rely on gravity to bring them back down; so sometimes the extensions stay elevated and are broken off by lawn mowers or passersby.

Rotary heads. These heads come in "pop-up" variety and are among the top-rated in uniform spreading of water. They are equipped with springs to draw the extended portion back in after use, and the structure of the more expensive brands is quite long-lasting and durable.

Each of the previously mentioned heads has a different design and variation depending on the brand, but the capacity of coverage is generally the same for each type.

About Leaky Pipe and Drip Systems

Many advertisements throughout the U.S. proclaim the benefits of a new and innovative technique of watering that uses less water and is much more effective at keeping a garden green and growing. These are leaky pipe systems and their derivatives. These watering systems are made up of thin lines of tubing that run *under* the surface of a garden and can supply plant roots directly with needed water.

The advantages of using such a system are as follows:

• Water is applied directly to roots in a continuous arrangement.

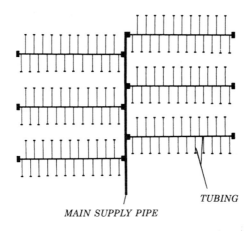

MAIN SUPPLY PIPE

TUBING

Leaky-pipe systems are also arranged flat underground in this pattern to water a large area. Tiny holes allow water to drip from the entire length of tubing that is not the main supply pipe.

- Fertilizer can be added to the water and distributed directly to the feeder roots without washing away or evaporating.
- Because water is fed directly to the roots without exposure to the sun or air, there is extremely little or no evaporation. This saves water and money.

In flower and vegetable gardens this procedure is an excellent way to distribute water to only the spots where plants are growing. But in states such as Arizona, New Mexico, Florida, and Utah (to name only a few) these drip systems have not yet been and are not likely to be perfected for the purpose of watering lawns. In these climates it is sometimes necessary to lay tubing in every square inch of a lawn to provide the correct water coverage. This is prohibitive with regard to both cost and function.

Before having one of these systems installed in your lawn, check with several sprinkler outfits to ensure that a drip system is feasible in your area.

Fields of Sprinkler System Coverage

To ensure that brown, yellow, and dead spots do not occur, the fields of spray for each head must be situated correctly to cover every square foot. Following are illustrations that exhibit desired sprinkler head placement.

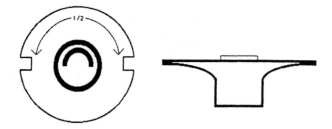

Standard orbit-type sprinkler head. These can be purchased in full, half, or quarter spray coverage.

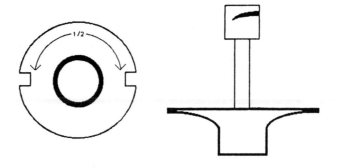

Pop-up orbit sprinkler heads can be set below the surface to keep heads from being easily damaged.

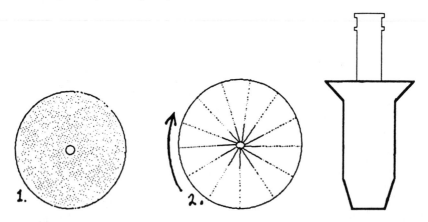

As shown in drawing 1, orbit-type heads spray in a broken pattern over their coverage area. Drawing 2 shows how a rotary head sprays broken streams. These streams rotate to soak the coverage area thoroughly.

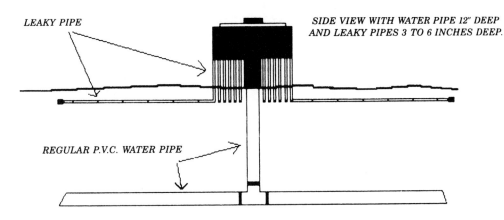

LEAKY PIPE

SIDE VIEW WITH WATER PIPE 12" DEEP
AND LEAKY PIPES 3 TO 6 INCHES DEEP.

REGULAR P.V.C. WATER PIPE

This is one variety of standard leaky-pipe system. Water is transferred to roots under the soil with no water loss from evaporation. This shows a side view with water pipe 12 inches deep and leaky pipes 3 to 6 inches deep.

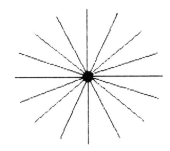

The leaky pipes are spread around the water dispenser in this star pattern.

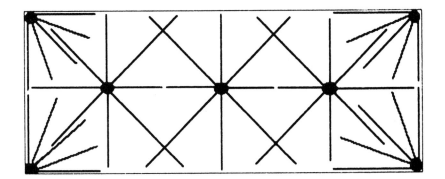

Leaky pipes are spread underground in an overlapping pattern.

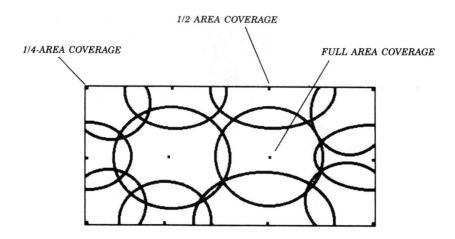

Some sprinkler head placements.

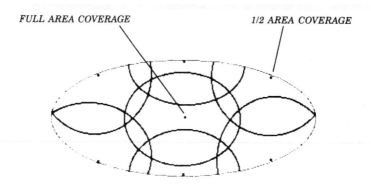

To cover an oddly shaped area it is sometimes necessary to overlap more than the area that needs to be watered.

Sprinkler Maintenance

It is virtually impossible *not* to break a sprinkler head at some point. But what must be remembered is that new heads can be replaced by *anyone* in just a few seconds, as long as pipes are not broken. If a pipe is broken, even if it is a main line; with PVC primer and glue, a repair job may actually take only five minutes!

A complete sprinkler repair kit (including pipe cutters, primer, glue, broken pipe insert remover, and a few elbows and tees) will cost only about twenty-five dollars.

It is important to clean dirt out of sprinkler heads and lines at least every two years to keep them functioning at peak efficiency.

NOTE: In my many years as a landscaper I have installed and had installed by other companies well over a hundred sprinkler systems. I have also repaired well over a thousand already established systems. The most common problem I encounter with repairing established systems is that when the now non-functioning system was first installed, the property owners used the lowest bidder for the installation. YOU WILL GET WHAT YOU PAY FOR! It is a very wise property owner that invests in a top-quality sprinkler system. Far too many times I have seen a property owner pay twice the amount of money to get a bad system fixed as the original bad system cost to install.

When it comes to the placement of heads, it is an absolute must for all heads to overlap one another. This ensures that your system will provide the type of coverage that keeps a lawn healthy and green.

When assessing the amount of pressure and deciding how many heads each sprinkler pressure valve will supply, ALWAYS underestimate. If your house has high pressure when you build your system, you can be sure that this pressure *will* decrease dramatically as the years pass. If you place too many heads per line, when the pressure decreases, your sprinkler system will no longer water your property adequately. Always be sure to use more lines and fewer heads per line no matter what the cost.

CHAPTER 5

Fertilizers

Though I chose the best strain of grass possible for long term effect for my own new lawn; though I used well researched planting procedures and kept up a regular watering routine, my lawn has continued to grow thicker and greener and more impressive because of the fertilizer I use, and how I regularly apply it.

Fertilizer is a substance that is added to soil to help plants grow. Just as a person takes food off of their shelves to make a meal, plants take nutrients out of soil to help them flourish. And, just as kitchen cupboards must be restocked when all of the food has been eaten, soil must be replenished when too many of the nutrients have been removed. As easy to understand as this principle seems, it was this replenishment factor that nearly did in the great plantations of the Old South. Many thousands of acres of rich farm soil were "burnt out" until the principle of crop rotation was utilized. In the Bible, the Israelites were ordered by their God to let crop fields lie fallow and unused for one out of seven seasons, specifically to allow the soil to be replenished. Landscapers, property owners, and homeowners lay down millions of tons of fertilizers every growing season throughout the world to force lawns to grow *thick* green base layers.

Fertilizers contain specific nutrients that are an absolute need for desirable plant growth. Some fertilizers are made from organic waste, such as manure or sewage. Others are manufactured from certain minerals or from synthetically refined compounds in factories. Annually, the amount spent on fertilizer reaches into the tens of billions of dollars.

WHAT IS IN FERTILIZER?

The process of *photosynthesis* (plants refining sunlight in order to produce energy for themselves) requires, in tandem, large amounts of nine chemical elements—carbon, hydrogen, oxygen, phosphorus, potassium, nitrogen, sulfur, calcium, and magnesium. It also requires smaller amounts of several other elements called micronutrients. Included among the micronutrients are boron, copper, zinc, iron, manganese, and molybdenum. Any successful fertilizer will contain various amounts of the most important of the preceding nine elements. What determines the differences among brands or types of fertilizer is often simply the mix of all these elements.

Fertlizer contents are designated by a three number sequence such as "21–3–3" or "16–16–16". These designations indicate the amounts of nitrogen, phosphorous, and potassium. But it is easier for the average person (even if it is not an *entirely* perfect analogy) to look at these numbers as representing above ground growth for the first number, root growth for the second number, and vitamin or *health* growth for the third number. Thus, a "21–3–3" means strong support for growth of the blades of grass, weak support for root growth, and weak support for the general health of the plant. This means that a "16–16–16" fertilizer supplies a level supply of the basic nutrients a plant needs. I myself have always found that the fertilizers with a high nitrogen count (the first number) and low second and third numbers, have caused my lawns to grow too fast and yet not get all that much thicker. For years I have been switching all of the lawns I maintain over to the use of 16–16–16 fertilizers.

Five years ago, all 16–16–16 fertilizer bags were labeled "Flower and Vegetable Garden Fertilizer." Now that the astounding results of the use of this composition of fertilizer have been demonstrated and publicized, you will see 16–16–16 bags labeled "Lawn & Garden Fertilizer."

One element that is essential for lawn growth, but is not supplied in most fertilizers is *iron*. Many lawns will remain a yellowish color and not green up no matter how much water and fertilizer is applied if iron is not added to the soil every three or four years. If a fertilizer label does not specifically state that iron is included, there will be no iron in the mix.

NOTE: In addition to general purpose fertilizers, there are many other additives for lawns. *Ironite* is a compound that primarily supplies iron nutrients to a lawn. *Gypsum* neutralizes alkali in soil. *Lime* neutralizes acid in soil.

KINDS OF FERTILIZER

There are basically two types of production fertilizers: *organic* and *mineral*.

Mineral Fertilizers

These are the most widely used fertilizers. They supply three main elements: nitrogen, phosphorus, and potassium.

Nitrogen Fertilizers. The most widely used mineral fertilizers are produced mainly from ammonia gas. Manufacturers use ammonia in making such liquid fertilizers as anhydrous ammonia and aqua ammonia. They also use it in producing solid fertilizers, such as ammonium sulfate, ammonium nitrate, ammonium phosphate, and an organic compound called urea.

Each of these fertilizers provides the soil with large amounts of nitrogen. Some of them, including ammonium sulfate and ammonium phosphate, furnish other elements as well.

Phosphorus Fertilizers. Called phosphates, these are made from the mineral apatite. Finely ground apatite may be applied to soil as a solid fertilizer called *rock phosphate.* Apatite also may be treated with sulfuric acid or phosphoric acid to make liquid fertilizers called *superphosphates.*

Potassium Fertilizers. These come largely from deposits of potassium chloride. Manufacturers mine these deposits of potash or extract them with water to produce such fertilizers as potassium chloride, potassium nitrate, and potassium sulfate.

Other Mineral Fertilizers. These provide soil with various elements. Those made from gypsum, for example, supply sulfur. Manufacturers also produce fertilizers that provide specific micronutrients.

Organic Fertilizers

Fertilizers can be comprised of a variety of organic substances, including manure, plant matter, sewage water, and packing house wastes. These fertilizers contain a smaller percentage of nutrients than do mineral fertilizers; therefore, they must be used in larger quantities to obtain the same results. Some organic fertilizers may also cost more, but they solve a disposal problem because organic waste has few uses other than as fertilizer. Plant matter becomes fertilizer most often in two ways—as compost or as green manure.

A Compost Pile consists of alternate layers of plant matter and soil. Fertilizer mixed with lime is also usually added. The pile is allowed to decay for several months before being used as fertilizer. When not mulching grass clippings back into the lawn as food, grass clippings added regularly to a compost pile help create excellent nitrogen rich deposits in your compost.

Green Manure consists of certain crops that farmers use as fertilizer. For example, some plants have bacteria in *nodules* (knot-like growths) on their roots. These bacteria take nitrogen directly out of the air and store it inside the stems and roots of the plant. Such plants, called *legumes,* include alfalfa, beans, and clover.

Farmers may plant a crop of legumes and then plow the young plants into the soil. As the plants decay, nitrogen returns to and enriches the soil so it can nourish other crops. As nitrogen is the element that is most used by plants in farm soils, the replenishment of nitrogen is of paramount importance.

Certain manufacturers have begun using these crops to produce a non-toxic organic fertilizer for homeowners to use on gardens and lawns. At this writing, these fertilizers can only be purchased at specialty stores, although their production and sale is becoming more prevalent all of the time.

Fertilizer Production

Fertilizer is produced in four basic forms.

1. **Straight goods fertilizer** is any chemical compound that contains one or two fertilizer elements.
2. **Bulk blend fertilizer** is a mixture of straight goods in specific proportions.
3. **Manufactured fertilizer** consists of two or more chemicals that are mixed and then formed into small grains. Each grain contains nitrogen, phosphorus, and potassium, and perhaps certain micronutrients.
4. **Liquid fertilizer** consists of one or more fertilizer materials dissolved in water. It may be sprayed on plants or soil, injected into soil, or added to irrigation water.

Most fertilizers release their nutrients into the soil almost immediately. Manufacturers also produce a special type of fertilizer called *slow-release fertilizer* that gives up its nutrients gradually. This type has been found useful when plants need a constant supply of nutrients over a long period of time.

Fertilizers with Weed Killers and Pesticides

Because pests and parasites have been developing immunities to what used to be lethal chemicals, and because many of the more successful chemicals have been taken off of the market for environmental reasons, fertilizers with pest controls are seldom sold anymore. Nor is an individual likely to find the application successful even if such a fertilizer were found and applied.

There are, however, many types of fertilizers that incorporate weed killers of all sorts. Although dual-purpose dry fertilizers do have some success in suppressing incursions of weeds in lawns and gardens, I have found that direct-purpose dry fertilizers work better when used in tandem with direct purpose spray weed killers.

In the case of spray fertilizers with a mixture of weed suppressant chemicals, however, the reports are quite different. I have found that there are few compounds and methods of distribution that can so quickly eliminate unsightly and tenacious weeds. But use of these additives is not without risk.

No matter what is stated by fertilizer manufacturers and companies that actively spread liquid fertilizer, high volumes of these additives are dangerous to children and animals. People in different parts of the country have reported wildlife leaving and not returning to areas that received fertilizer treatments with weed killer additives. Still other unsubstantiated reports have told of dogs getting sick and dying soon after the spraying of a formula that contains pesticides.

It is wise to regulate carefully the amount of fertilizer with pesticide and weed killer additives or to be sure to water heavily soon after an application. If you're ever in doubt, check with an authority to verify the toxicity and potency of a particular additive.

METHODS OF FERTILIZATION

There are basically three methods used for laying down fertilizer on a lawn.

1. Manually spreading a large amount (usually what is recommended on a fertilizer package) once or twice a year.
2. Having a company spray a liquid fertilizer on an average of once a month.
3. Hand spreading small amounts on a biweekly or weekly basis.

Manually Spreading A Large Amount (Dry Fertilizer)

This is perhaps the least effective of the three methods of fertilizing. Usually a person employs a drop spreader to disperse the amount of fertilizer that is recommended on the package of the purchased product. With a rolling drop spreader an individual has little or no control over the amount of fertilizer that falls to the ground—particularly when rolling over a bumpy lawn or troublesome roots. At every bump or hole the drop spreader can release too much fertilizer and the result is all kinds of burned spots that take months for a lawn to repair on its own, if ever.

Even if a drop spreader is not used, and a large amount of fertilizer is spread on a lawn by another method such as broadcast spreading, burn spots can easily occur. These show up within days as yellow areas of dead grass blades.

Studies have shown that a large amount of fertilizer applied all at once results in a great deal of waste. A lawn can only use so much food in a given amount of time. The rest will either evaporate or wash away, doing your lawn no good whatsoever.

The last problem with a large amount of fertilizer spread manually only once or twice a year is that your grass seems to suddenly grow too fast and too long, and it almost becomes necessary to mow twice a week for a solid month. Then, when the month is over, your lawn is back to normal (thin and no longer as green), and may seem as if no benefit was derived except to increase your exercise program. The only recognized benefits are the low cost involved, some root growth and some lasting greening effects.

Having A Company Spray Fertilizer

The effectiveness of this method is about medium when it comes to greening and maintaining a lawn but is first-rate in removing weeds. Few burn spots occur, although this depends on the reliability of the company called upon to do the job. In fact, this whole system depends on the reliability of the company dealt with, and this reliability can only be certified by reputation or time. You can always try an outfit and cancel if they do not work out.

Based on the work of a good company, the benefits are

- excellent and quick removal of weeds
- medium to good greening
- fast dispersal of fertilizer to a lawn's root system
- no effort involved

Possible problems with this system are as follows:

1. As all companies caution against children and animals playing on a lawn for a period of one to three days after spraying, there is a toxic risk with this method.
2. It has been reported that as much as half of the amount of fertilizer sprayed down may wash away with no benefit to the lawn. Although

these reports have not been substantiated, if as much as half is washing away, a great amount of money is being wasted.

3. In most cases a sprayed lawn will grow fast (causing a more frequent need for mowing) for three weeks and then go back to normal until the next treatment. This is certainly not desirable.

4. These treatments for an average size lawn through a commercial company are by far the most expensive of the three methods.

Hand Spreading Small Amounts

This method is by far the most time- and cost-efficient procedure. You must first figure the amount of fertilizer needed for your lawn over an average growing period. To do this, figure three cups of fertilizer for 1,000 square feet of lawn area. If the growing season is twenty-eight weeks a year, the formula is 28×3 cups (1,000 ft).

When the entire amount needed for a typical season has been calculated, divide this amount by the number of times you anticipate cutting the lawn. For example, if you usually mow your lawn once a week and there are 22 weeks of cutting a year, divide the total amount of fertilizer by 22. Apply this small amount each week after mowing the lawn by using either a push broadcast spreader or a hand-held broadcast spreader. Make sure that all the fertilizer is evenly spread throughout the lawn area. Finally, water the entire applied surface.

There are many benefits to this method.

1. Because of the small amount used, no burn spots occur.

2. The cost of fertilizing is only a fraction of that of the next best method.

3. There is little or no danger of toxicity to animals or children.

4. It is root growth that determines the health, depth, and lushness of a lawn. With these regular applications the root system of a lawn feeds regularly and grows steadily and strongly.

5. Very little washes away; thus the entire benefit of the fertilizer is realized.

6. An extremely small amount of time is required.

7. Your grass is not getting so much fertilizer that it grows too fast and needs to be cut more frequently than your regular mowing schedule.

NOTE: Over a 16-year period, testing on hundreds of lawns, I have never obtained better results than when I applied small amounts of fertilizer each week after mowing a lawn. The results of this method are so good that these lawns became like thick shag carpets of green; anyone walking on them would sink into the thatch base for an inch and a half. No matter how diligent the companies were that applied fertilizer in other ways, their lawns could never compare with the appearance of the lawns that were fed regularly with small amounts each week.

CHAPTER
6

Lawn Mowers & Lawn Mowing

Whether you establish your own lawn or purchase a property that already has a lawn, the most frequent and long-term activity you will be doing on your lawn is not playing on it or picnicking on it. No, your most frequent interaction will be the wonderful, exhilarating experience of mowing it. With all of the time you will be spending on this weekly event, it is best to make sure that this exciting activity is as smooth and easy as possible.

MOWER TYPES

Reel Lawn Mowers

Although these types were once more common than any other, today you have the best chance of sighting them in a garage, rummage, or yard sale. Most of them are of the push (manual) type, but several have been manufactured with engines and power drive.

Reel mowers cut extremely well because of the particular action they utilize that cuts the grass between two surfaces. The particular way these machines are built also helps draw the grass onto the cutting surface regardless of lawn length—something few lawn mowers can do as well.

Reel mowers are not seen very often anymore for several reasons.

1. Most people prefer power mowers over manual types. Most reel mowers sold today are manual.

2. Power reel mowers are not built with a direct shaft drive; so a breakdown of chain or engine can frequently occur.

Simple reel lawn mower, manual style.

3. There are many blades to be sharpened on a reel, and since the sharpening process is difficult, the time involved is much greater than for other lawn mowers.

4. Because the blade is exposed, many government agencies have publicized these mowers as unsafe. Certainly, there have been many documented reports of objects such as small rocks and sprinkler heads being thrown directly and with great force back at reel mower operators.

5. When blades become chipped or cracked beyond repair (a common occurrence with all lawn mowers), it is about five times more expensive to replace a reel blade.

Power-driven reel lawn mower.

Simple Rotary Blade Push Lawn Mower

Simple rotary lawn mowers are the most commonly used at this time, though self-propelled types are quickly catching up.

Simple rotary mowers are the cheapest to manufacture and the most inexpensive to maintain. They come in different varieties, such as side baggers, rear baggers, and high vacuum baggers. Most people prefer rear baggers because of the convenience of not having to maneuver a machine with a bag sticking far out to the side. But side baggers are excellent cutting machines in other ways. As a rule, they are considerably cheaper to buy and breakdowns are few and far between with little care and maintenance required.

High vacs are best at cutting. The way the undercarriage and grass funnels are shaped causes the grass to be sucked up (standing straight) so that it can be cut evenly, leaving an excellent appearance.

Rotary lawn mower with side bagger attachment.

Simple rotary rear-bagger.

All of these except the high vacs come in gas or electric power. Though the electrics do not usually have the power of gas-run models, they are extremely quiet and light to handle. When an electric model breaks down, however, repairs can be difficult and expensive.

Self-Propelled Rotary

These models, though they do not necessarily cut better than any previously mentioned, can be very convenient.

If a lawn has hills, a self-propelled mower reduces the difficulty by a third! And on a flat and even lawn, time is cut by 25 percent.

After 16 years of cutting lawns, I would not mow another without a good self-propelled lawn mower to keep me going. If you are planning on getting a self-propelled model, however, it is well worth paying more for the better quality models. These move faster and work longer without breaking down. The deck of an expensive machine is designed to maximize air flow, which in turn maximizes even and clean cutting.

It has been my experience that even with minimal use, self-propelled models that are cheaply sold at local hardware stores instead of the mower specialty shops will seldom be worth buying and using. The wear and tear on cheaply made drive systems is so great that most do not last beyond two years. On the other hand, well made and higher priced models are known to work a good seven years or more without significant problems.

One cautionary note: If there is a breakdown with a self-propelled model, the greater number of moving parts that make up the drive can be very expensive and difficult to replace. A good warranty is a must!

POWER CLUTCH HAND BAR.

Standard self-propelled rear bagger.

A mulcher mower has a blade specifically designed to chew grass cuttings into small pieces that are left on a lawn.

Another advantage of certain of these models is a feature called a *blade clutch.* This stops the blade when the handle is released, but leaves the engine running. It saves wear on fingers and ignition systems. Also, on certain models this clutch will upgrade the power of a 3 horsepower engine to better than that of a 4 horsepower on a regular rear bagger—a wonderful feature.

Mulcher Mower

Developed over the last ten years into a workable and reliable standard, the mulcher mower is becoming quite popular throughout the United States. This mower either has no bag and a sealed deck, or it has an insert that seals off the mower deck so that no grass is thrown up and out. The specially designed action of the blade throws the cut grass up into the deck where it bounces back into the blades to be cut again. When the grass has been bounced around between the mower blades and the deck enough times to resemble sawdust, the grass will fall back onto the lawn to be absorbed efficiently into the lawn as nitrogen rich fertilizer.

This mower will work well on just about any variety of grass as long as a few rules are carefully followed. The deck must be kept clean or the action cannot work correctly. If the grass is wet at all from dew, sprinklers or rain, the blades will be too heavy to be thrown up and bounced around. The drier the grass the better the mulching works. During the peak growing seasons of fall and spring, when the blades of grass are long, they will again be too heavy to be thrown around and cut up sufficiently. Therefore, during these times in the season, if you use a mulcher, you will have to cut the lawn twice a week. Having to mow twice a week definitely puts a damper on owning a mulcher mower.

Commercial Extrawide Walk Behind or Ride Behind

This mower comes standard with the self-propelled feature and is extremely useful for cutting very large lawns. It is easy to maneuver extremely tight turns, but of course is very difficult to get through small gates or garages. Blades are easy to sharpen and repairs are not called for very often. Most, however, are not equipped with bags to pick up the grass.

If an individual owned a field-size lawn, or wanted to cut professionally, one of these mowers is a must to own. Though expensive to buy, breakdowns are seldom and the time spent mowing large expanses is cut down to a fraction.

Riding Lawn Mower

As a rule, riders have a large turning radius, making them impractical for any but the larger lawns. And even people with big lawns have trouble getting a rider to both front and back yards.

If an individual owns a private yard—fenced and enclosed; then, access is usually only through a gate or garage. A rider is far too large to fit through either of these in most cases. Also, only a few of them (usually the most expensive) have bags to pick up the cut grass.

Yet when you have a large lawn and there is available access, there really is no substitute for a riding lawn mower. They involve so little effort. They can be adapted for many purposes, such as snow removal and garden hoeing or even equipment towing. When a rider is indicated, do not hesitate to purchase one and save yourself time and effort.

Standard riding lawn mower.

Which Mowing Machines Make A Lawn Look Good?

Many people wonder about whether an inexpensive mower can make a lawn look as good as an expensive one can. The answer to this is, yes, it is possible and very likely that a lawn mowed by an inexpensive machine will look as good. In long years of experience, however, I have found that the biggest liability of inexpensive machines is that they fall apart. The expensive lawn mowers that I personally use mow more lawns in three days than a typical home owner's mower would have to mow in a whole season, and yet these models last me four years.

Following are several factors that determine how well a cut lawn looks (in order of importance):

- *Sharpness of the blade.* If a blade *cuts* your grass instead of tearing, bending, and bruising, then your lawn will look good.

- *Steadiness and evenness of the wheels.* If the wheels are not steady, then at different points the grass is cut short and a few inches farther away it is cut long. This effect is very noticeable on even an unhealthy thin lawn, let alone a healthy thick one.

- *Vacuum ability.* If a mower is built well and causes the grass to stand up, the cut will be even and smooth over the entire lawn surface.

- *Speed of blade.* Fast blade action causes grass to stand up, thus cutting it straighter and smoother. Faster blades also cut rather than bruise and tear. Unfortunately, faster blades are usually associated with more powerful engines, which usually only come with more expensive models.

- *Horsepower of engine.* If a lawn is thick, wet, or just long, an engine with lower horsepower will bog down and slow up, causing the grass to be cut poorly. Unless an engine has a power up-grading clutch, never buy a gas mower with less than 3.5 horsepower. Five horsepower is much, much more preferable.

What Am I Looking for in a Lasting Mower?

Tests have shown that lawn mowers tend to develop the same problems in certain areas. When purchasing a mower model, make certain that these problem areas have been addressed and eliminated.

Wheels. Far too often machines are manufactured with plastic wheels that tend to break. All-metal wheel rims are best. Poor attachment of wheels to the lawn mower deck is another *big* problem. Buying a machine that uses wheel axles or solid steel mountings eliminates this difficulty.

Handles. Maneuvering a mower around trees, gardens, and sidewalks causes strain on a mower handle, even if the mower is self-propelled. If a handle is collapsible, the metal becomes cracked and breaks directly at the joint. Look for strong, tight bolts and thick metal handles. If you grab a mower display model by the handle and the handle "shimmys" at all, you can bet that in a relatively short time it will begin to experience metal fatigue and break off.

Bent motor shafts. If a mower has a long, thin motor shaft, the first time a hidden rock or tough sprinkler head is clipped, the shaft will bend and the mower will become absolutely useless. Buy a mower with a thick, short shaft. Most mowers are fitted with a soft metal "key" to prevent this from happening, but the blades are moving so quickly that this safety measure does not always work. Unfortunately, this feature can be hard to check for.

Pull ropes. These days lawn mowers are fitted by law with an engine cutoff switch at the handle to prevent injury by a moving blade. You let go of the handle and the motor goes off. This measure, however, causes more frequent use of the pull rope because every time you empty the catcher you have to stop the mower, and it has to be restarted. When the pull rope breaks, repairs are frustrating. Search for thicker and better-designed ropes.

Bag attachments. Most grass catchers are made out of metal rods and cloth. If this cloth is thin, the moisture in grass blades will cause bacteria to grow that will eat through the bag. If the rods are too thin, they will bend under the weight of the grass and break. These bag attachments can cost as much to replace as a quarter of the entire cost of the mower. Search for a model with thick cloth, heavy rods, and plenty of support for the bag. Also, make sure

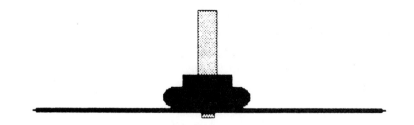

Motor shafts that are long and skinny will break if something is struck accidentally. Look for thick shafts that are not too long.

that no part of the rod frame is pressing sharply up against the bag. These areas will wear through very soon.

Cylinder sleeve. To manufacture engines less expensively many companies cast small engine cylinder housings in aluminum. But aluminum expands and contacts very easily and soon the piston rings cannot fill their required space to keep the oil in the engine from burning. To alleviate this problem, well-built engines are manufactured with cast-iron sleeves that do not expand as much. Ask whether the mower you have chosen has one of these cast-iron sleeves.

Cutting-height adjustment. Whether expensive or inexpensive, rider or walker, self-propelled or manual, make certain that any model purchased has a cutting-height adjustment that can be manipulated easily. *Do not* purchase a

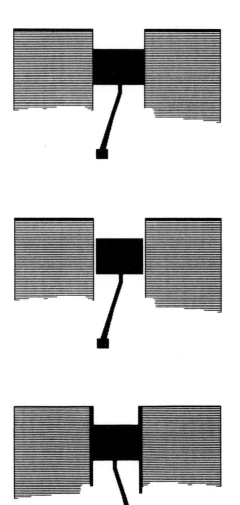

Most engine blocks are made of aluminum, which will expand and contract greatly with heat and cold.

With the expansion and contraction a gap will form and oil will escape into the combustion chamber. Power is lost this way and an engine will soon break down.

Cast-iron sleeves in a cylinder housing will contract and expand less. Such an engine will have double the life of a normal aluminum engine.

mower without this feature. Much trouble and damage to a lawn can be saved with adherence to this suggestion. All lawns are different and are grown under individual conditions. To be able to cut a lawn at the optimum height, wheel adjustments are essential.

CUTTING LAWNS

Proper mowing management is an essential part of keeping a lawn healthy and green. With proper thought and planning great amounts of time and effort are saved and your lawn will thrive, remaining lush and green throughout the growing season.

How High Should I Cut?

The first mowing in the spring should be thought of as the "cleanup" mowing. At this time the correctly determined amount of lawn should be removed to guard against the growth of fungus diseases. A power rake (discussed in a following chapter) may be necessary.

Set your lawn mower to an inch in height, taking time to cut out and remove dead grass. Never leave the lawn mower at a one-inch setting for more than the first two or three cuttings. As the weather gets hot, the blade should be raised to anywhere from 1½ inches to 2 inches, depending on climate, variety of grass, and personal preference. With most varieties of grass, the higher you can stand to cut, the healthier the lawn will look.

Why High Cutting?

The height to which grass should be cut depends chiefly on the kind grown. Yet over the long period, higher cutting gives you the following benefits:

- It encourages deeper rooting.
- It reduces surface evaporation and lowers your water bill.
- It takes some of the force out of the water drops from large-volume sprinklers and thereby prevents erosion.
- It keeps roots shaded and weed seeds from sprouting.
- It is the most effective and inexpensive way to control crabgrass because crabgrass has a difficult time seeding and sprouting in the shade of a thick mat of grass.

How Often Should I Cut?

Frequent cutting is essential if you want to keep your lawn uniformly green. If the grass grows too tall between mowings, the green foliage will be mowed off, leaving mostly stems that are yellowed from being shaded. Grass that is mowed frequently always has sufficient foliage remaining to keep it looking freshly green and to aid the growth of deeper, more abundant roots.

Ornamental gardens are mowed as often as twice a week during the height of the growing season. But regular homeowners need cut only once a week.

Some lawns can go for as long as two weeks, but generally these do not look as good as a lawn that is cut on a more regular basis. So even if a lawn is slow growing, it is recommended that it be cut no less frequently than every ten days.

Should I Leave the Clippings?

This is a hard question to answer. Many case histories can be cited to prove that either leaving or removing clippings is best. So the real question is, *Do I have a particular lawn that will or will not benefit from leaving the grass clippings?*

If your lawn is deep and flexible with a good thick thatch base, it would be better to catch the clippings. If your lawn is sparse, with dirt showing in between, or even if the dirt is well covered by green grass but the thatch base is thin and you have lots of traffic, it would be beneficial to leave the clippings.

Clippings only do harm when they are left in clumps and piles. These clumps burn the grass when the sun comes out and leave yellow spots just as if a dog had left his calling card.

If you wish to let the grass clippings remain on the lawn, be sure to do this when the clippings are short so they can work down into the grass and form a light mulch to feed the lawn.

In a low-humidity climate, grass clippings do not readily decay but rather settle around the stolons (main moisture-absorbing roots), forming an impermeable thatch that resists penetration of water and fertilizer. Also, under summer conditions of moisture and heat, matted grass clippings foster the development of fungus diseases and form a breeding place for sod webworms.

So, the question still begs to be asked, "Should I mulch clippings or should I bag them?" In my experience, after weighing in on all of the facts listed above, I usually recommend to mulch whenever possible. Just make sure that the conditions for mulching are right and that absolutely no clumps of cut grass blades are left anywhere. If your mulcher mower cannot do the job without leaving clumps of grass, bag the grass instead.

Lawn-Mowing Patterns

As a mower rolls over a lawn, its tires lightly crush and bend the blades of grass to create an unmistakable pattern of cutting. Also, since the blade is cutting one certain direction when the mower is heading forward, to turn sharply back at the end of a cut and return side by side to the last cut will create a different corridor of blade-cutting direction. This pattern can be seen in a lawn for quite some time, depending on the geographic location and density of the lawn being cut. Patterns can be arranged in some very attractive designs. Whenever I watch an outdoor football game either in person or on the television, I always take note of how clearly the crisscross pattern of the cutting shows up.

Simple Square Cut. This is done by running the lawn mower in a straight up-and-down direction one week and the next week running side to side.

Diamond Cut. Here the lawn mower is run straight back and forth at a diagonal direction for one week and at the opposite diagonal direction the next week.

Run the lawn mower straight in one direction on the first week and straight in the other direction the next week. The result will be a checkerboard.

Run a lawn mower at one angle the first week and the other angle the next week.

S-curve cut. To accomplish this, simply follow a uniform S-curve throughout the entire cutting of the lawn.

CHAPTER
7

Edging a Lawn

Mowing is the bigger job and will take a lot longer to conclude once started, but edging is what makes the job look finished and professional. Wherever I mow lawns, neighbors come up to me and ask, "Why does your cutting job look so much better than mine? My lawn mower is as good as yours, and I have been mowing all of my life. What am I doing wrong? What makes the difference?" The secret lies in creating perfect edges around the entire lawn, including along the garden and any walks or driveways.

In life, our boundaries define who we are. Boundaries say what we will do and what we will not do. People judge us by our boundaries. When it comes to our yards, people judge how well our lawn looks by how well the boundaries (or edges) are defined. Take a look at any gardening magazine and you will observe that the featured gardens have definite and highly visible edges. Over the many years I have worked with lawns, real-estate agents and home owners have frequently asked me to help prepare homes for sale. Often the only thing I do to get the home to sell is to create a perfect edge all around the lawn.

To make your lawn the envy of the neighborhood, create great edges and maintain them regularly with a few minutes of work each week. The perfect edge consists of perfect right angles. To achieve this perfect edge, a variety of tools, both manual and powered, can be used.

EDGING EQUIPMENT

Though there are other edging tools on the market, I am featuring only those that, after sixteen years of testing, I have found to be of value.

Edger Tool No matter how high-powered and high-tech my equipment gets, I always find use for this tool and am glad I have it. If you have a flower or vegetable garden that has been invaded by your lawn, this tool is just about the only thing I have found to do the job of establishing a clean edge and clearing out the in-grown grass. Make sure that the model you buy is equipped with a strong handle to withstand the strain of prying up grass by the roots.

Weed-Eater-Style Blade Edger For professionals and homeowners alike this tool will save time and maintain a great edge. In order for this tool to work properly, an edge must already be created and dug out by a powerful ground-based edger. Because they are not powerful enough, if you try to create a new edge with this tool, you will only waste a lot of time and effort. Yet, when an edge has been created, nothing makes a cleaner right angle edge than this weed-eater-style powered blade edger.

Gas-Powered Ground-Based Edger When a lawn edge has been neglected for a year or two, it often grows three or four inches out onto the sidewalk and driveway. Because grass has an affinity for lime and calcium, it grows out onto concrete whenever possible and tries to leach these compounds out of the hard surface. The most efficient way to cut through these "grass snakes" is to use a gas powered rolling edger. These machines have a steel blade that will cut a perfect straight edge through the toughest soil and sod.

Once I have cut an edge, I do not use this machine to keep an edge maintained. The reason for this is that the blades are very powerful and thus, very dangerous. It is not that the blade will fly off (at least not in my experience), but the debris thrown off is another matter. Rocks, dust, sand and even sprinkler heads that might be hidden along the lawn edge (a perfect place for sprinkler heads to be placed) can be thrown thirty feet or more. One employee of mine hit a sprinkler head by accident and the head crashed through a second story window. Because of this flying debris, I never let anyone watch when I cut an edge, and I make certain that no vehicles are parked nearby. Depending on the brand of the machine, the replacement blades can be very expensive, and they wear down quickly. To save on operating costs, I only use this machine when nothing else will do.

I have some lawn that I have mowed for over ten years straight. Most all of these lawns had an edge put on them by this large machine *only* when I first mowed them a decade ago. Since then the edges have remained perfect by using only the weed-eater blade and string trimmer type devices.

Gas-Powered String Trimmer Next to the weed-eater style blade edger, this device is my most frequently used edging tool. Wherever I go, I see homeowners who are already familiar with, and are frequently using, this machine. For trimming grass blades along buildings and ornamental borders that the lawn mower cannot get to, this tool is perfect. Many uninformed property owners, however, try to use it for re-establishing a neglected edge, or maintaining edges along walks and drives. This is not a good idea. As my wife and I go for walks through nice manicured neighborhoods, we make bets with each other on who uses a string trimmer for edging. The butchered, rounded shape of the edge gives it away every time.

As a professional with long experience, I have learned to turn my string trimmer upside down and use it to create the desired perfect right angle edge. But after repeated failed attempts to teach the average person this technique, I have found it better to just recommend the weed-eater style blade edger to maintain perfect right angle edges.

DECORATIVE BORDERS

At times, grass can seem as if it is in possession of a sort of perverse intelligence or even a kind of belligerence. Property owners carefully create and prepare perfect landscapes for a lawn to grow in. They bring in special soil, they fertilize, they water, they weed. And yet, in spite of this care, sometimes the grass simply won't do very well. Meanwhile, some of these same property owners create flower gardens and vegetable gardens that inevitably become inundated with hearty grass colonies. In short, grass just doesn't seem to want to grow where you *want* it to, only where you *don't* want it to.

One of the best ways to keep grass from growing past your established edge and into a garden is by installing decorative borders. Many people I have met have installed such borders and cannot understand how the grass still grows past them into the garden. This is because borders are only a deterrent to grass, not a complete preventive. The deeper and more established the border, however, the better the deterrent works.

In addition to keeping grass in check, borders can and should be very decorative. Borders make a yard look professionally landscaped like no other detail can.

Concrete borders A trend over the last ten years has been to have companies bring in curbing machines to create graceful, flowing curbs around the entire lawn edge bordering gardens or flower beds. These companies come in, cut a shallow trough, remove the sod and dirt, and use a machine that mixes and lays down the concrete on the spot. Though this curbing practice is done so much that it has almost become blasé to see, it creates an efficient, practical and aesthetic border.

Plastic Border and curbing Though this material is sold to thousands of people around the country every day, it is the most inefficient material that can be used. The best feature of plastic borders is that the material is cheap to purchase and can be placed down by anyone. It has been my experience, however, that the material curls up in the heat of summer and no longer looks good. Because the plastic is so flexible, grass colonies can too easily push against the plastic, eventually warping the border into shapes that are something less than perfect. The end result is high maintenance and more work.

Railroad Ties These large blocks of wood soaked in creosote are used to create lawn borders and build high standing flower beds and even retaining walls. I have found these tie borders to be extremely durable and easy to install. Ties are usually quite thick so they can be placed deep, and they are heavy so there is no question of them being pushed around by the grass. Many people, though, believe that railroad ties are a little bit too rough and unrefined looking.

Brick borders Brick is available in many different shapes and colors that can be used for lawn and garden borders or retaining walls. Depending on the type of border, the bricks may or may not need to be cemented or mortared into place.

Brick borders last for a long time, making them economical and efficient. Some bricks can be buried deep and stacked high, which keeps them from being pushed back or overwhelmed by the grass. Some brick styles have to be mortared to work efficiently, and though these are more difficult to get set in place, mortared borders are both beautiful and long lasting.

The most common border is just the trimmed edge of grass. This edge is simple—and when maintained—quite beautiful too. But edges without decorative borders take the most effort to keep up and are easily overrun. Re-establishing overrun borders is a difficult and time-consuming job, while maintaining an established edge takes only a few short minutes each week. Since a good edge is essential for a great looking lawn, the maintenance route is definitely the best way to go.

CHAPTER
8

Aeration

E ach spring my phone lines are flooded with calls from customers asking me to aerate their lawns. This is wonderful for me because it provides plenty of work after the inactive winter months, and it is wonderful for them because, on a maintenance level, nothing I know of helps a lawn keep itself in peak condition like regular aeration. The problem is, spring is the only time I get this flood of calls for aeration, and yet it is a job that should be done a minimum of three times a year.

Aeration involves creating a large number of small holes in a lawn in order to give the roots access to air, water, and fertilizer. Though there are hand tools available for this purpose, I strongly recommend the use of an aeration machine, which can be rented, or that you have a professional come and do the job.

Good aerators make between ten and twelve holes per square foot of lawn surface. There are two different ways aerators will make these holes. One way is to use solid spikes on a roller to forcefully punch holes in the ground, pushing back soil to make a vacant space. Another will force hollow shafts on a roller into the soil, thus removing plugs of sod, root, and dirt. Most groundskeepers prefer the second type because it makes the holes without compacting the soil surrounding them. Also, the hollow shaft aerator always penetrates deeper.

HOW AERATION HELPS A LAWN

Anyone who has ever tended a garden of any kind knows that if it is not tilled and hoed to break up the soil, the garden surface will soon become so hard that the garden plants will be unable to grow. Hard soil chokes the life out of plants. If you till the soil and break it up though, your plants seem to spring up from the ground and say "Wow, you saved my life!" Garden soils get hard and compact only from the action of wind and water; they hardly ever need suffer through traffic.

But lawns not only have wind, rain, and sun to contend with, they must also endure the dogs, cats and humans trafficking across them daily. Unfortunately, and quite obviously, you cannot till a lawn as you would a garden. So what you do to simulate tilling is to aerate your lawn thoroughly and regularly.

When plugs are removed by aeration they should be left on a lawn to be absorbed back into the grass. The organic half of the plugs will act as quality fertilizer to feed the lawn as they are organically broken down. With each successive watering the dirt clinging to a plug will wash into the ground and mix quickly back into the topsoil. Lawn cutting helps to reduce these plugs more quickly and easily by chopping them up into a size that breaks down faster. It is best not to leave clay based plugs too long without a good watering because they will bake hard in the sun and require the action of continued wind, weather, watering, and mowing to break them down completely.

The holes left by aeration serve a variety of extremely useful purposes.

1. *Increased root growth.* In hard soil where lawn roots can barely penetrate the surface, a space is created when the plugs are removed that will be easily filled by new lawn roots. When it comes to grass, increased density and depth of lawn roots means greener and more luxuriant growth. An aerator that does not remove plugs defeats this purpose. If the soil around a hole is packed harder and more densely than before aeration, lawn roots will have a harder time growing into and filling these holes.

2. *Decreased water evaporation.* In areas composed mostly of hard packed soils or clay, water tends to remain on the surface and thus evaporates more quickly, leaving grass dry or dead. Aeration holes (usually from one to three inches deep) create a sponge effect with thousands of tiny reservoirs that draw water down below the surface.

3. *Increased watershed.* Where lawns grow on a slope and water runs off because of gravity (regardless of soil makeup) these holes create a substantial and desirable watershed as each hole allows water to sink in instead of flowing off the slope. Regular aeration can save up to 30 percent of evaporation and runoff on a slope!

4. *Increased oxygen to soil.* Aeration holes allow oxygen to reach lawn roots more easily, promoting thicker and greener growth. When soil compaction is too great to allow enough oxygen below the surface or when the same compaction keeps water from draining rapidly enough, earthworms rise to the surface on a regular basis. The mounds left by these worms are most easily recognized because of the feel of marbles under-

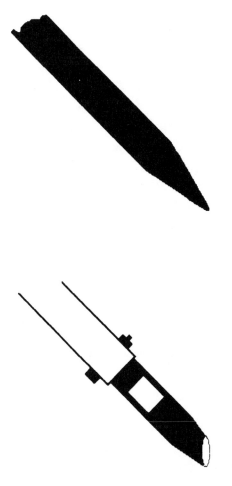

This is a standard aerator rod that pushes back the soil and leaves a hole. This type of rod (along with about thirty others of the same size) can be attached to a large heavy wheel, or it can be attached with three others to a piston-type assembly depending on the machine that is used.

This is a standard aerator shaft that will remove plugs of sod, roots, and soil. This can also be attached to a rolling wheel with about thirty similar shafts, or it can be attached to pistons with three others, depending on the machine used.

foot when walking on a lawn. Regular aeration lets more air down into the soil, causing worms to rise to the surface less frequently since oxygen is what worms want, and thus leaves the lawn smoother and more even.

5. *Elimination of fungus.* When water is not able to drain through the surface of a lawn, pooling or congealing instead, fungus spores are able to gain a hold from airborne seeding. Once the seeding has taken place, the non-draining water enables the fungus to become prolific and spread. Aeration holes allow water to drain through matted lawns and tough surface dirt, removing the supportive environment that the spores need.

6. *Increased fertilizer utilization.* A lawn benefits greatly when applied fertilizer is able to get directly and quickly to the roots. On hard soils, applied fertilizer can wash away before it reaches the roots. Aerator holes can be thought of as thousands of holding bins that retain fertilizer up to

three times longer. This saves money and produces a more beautiful and valuable lawn!

WHEN IS AERATION INDICATED?

Very few lawns cannot benefit from correct and frequent aeration. Yet there are a number of signs that give specific indication of need.

Hard Soil With Thin Grass

In this instance water is evaporating, fertilizer is being washed off, and roots cannot easily spread. Free oxygen exchange is also cut off. Any yard that has animals and children frequently crossing over, running on, or playing on the grass surfaces will have this condition to one extent or another.

Sensation of Walking on Marbles Just Under the Lawn Surface

This condition is caused by earthworms pushing up holes in the lawn and indicates a lack of oxygen exchange in the soil. This symptom can also indicate difficulty in water drainage past the surface.

Sloping Grounds

The problem here is water runoff. Water runs off all slopes to some extent, but regular aeration slows this runoff and helps lessen the extent to which the grass gets dried out.

HOW OFTEN SHOULD YOU AERATE?

Golf courses have the most expert groundskeepers in the world working to keep the course as perfect as possible. Most courses are aerated every month. But because residential properties usually do not have the high traffic volume that golf courses do, I recommend they be aerated three times per year—once in the spring to help keep the rains, runoff and fertilizer in the ground; once in the summer to help soil that is baked and rock hard to hold water; and again during the fall to drain water past the surface and keep fungus from gaining a hold.

Beginning in the last century, we have developed expectations for our lawn grass that run counter to the natural growing cycles.

Under natural conditions most grasses are dormant during winter and summer and experience peak growth in spring and fall. The problem is that with the exception of winter, we expect three seasons of lush and green lawn, even through the worst heat of summer. To achieve this, we water frequently and fertilize often, tricking the lawn into thinking it is spring and fall during the summer months. Regular aeration helps considerably to stimulate peak period growth.

CONTRAINDICATIONS

Don't aerate the following:

1. New lawns, just planted;
2. shade lawns that have large amounts of dirt showing;

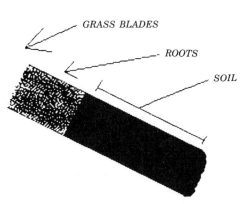

An aeration plug, shown same size, taken under excellent conditions. If the ground is hard or dry, the plug will be considerably smaller.

GRASS BLADES

ROOTS

SOIL

Water, fertilizer, or needed insecticides will gather inside the aeration holes and stay long enough to benefit a lawn.

3. grass growing sparsely, appearing only in clumps;

4. soil that is composed of light gravel and sand.

Lawns with conditions 1, 2, and 3 will only be torn up by aerator machines, negating any possible benefit. Water drains right through those with condition 4, often without giving a lawn nearly the amount of necessary moisture. Aeration will only make this water drain faster.

Remember:

You can maximize aeration by *preparing* the ground with a thorough watering.

Aeration can be done at any time during the year because of the varied and generous results. The only restriction will be if the ground is too hard because it is frozen or too dry.

CHAPTER
9

Power Raking

The breeding and genetic enchancement of lawn strains to create specific cultivated varieties has side effects that we as property owners must work around. One side effect of making strains that will stay green all year with regular fertilization and watering is that the portion of sod called the "thatch base" often overgrows and becomes too thick.

This thick thatch is difficult to mow because the mower sinks down into it and cannot roll well. Such a base of overgrowth is also difficult to water well because it acts like a sponge, soaking up the water before it gets down to the roots where it is really needed. This thatch base also gives up water very quickly when the sun beats down in the heat of the day. The only way to remove thatch without harming the lawn or spending hour upon hour of backbreaking labor is to use a power rake.

A power rake is a machine with many free-swinging "keys" that spin at a rate of 18 to 30 revolutions per second. As these keys rotate and strike a lawn, they cut up a portion of the thick intertwining of stolons and surface roots and attached dead grass blades that comprise the thatch and force this matter to the surface where it can be picked up and hauled away.

The keys also have sharpened corners that slice into the sod for surface aeration. In this way, some of the advantages of aerating are produced by a power rake, albeit on a much smaller scale.

LAWN MOWER ATTACHMENTS

There is a power rake attachment on the market that can be affixed to rotary lawn mowers. This product supposedly enables you to power rake your lawn as efficiently as a regular machine but at a fraction of the cost of either buying a dedicated power rake or having someone do the job for you.

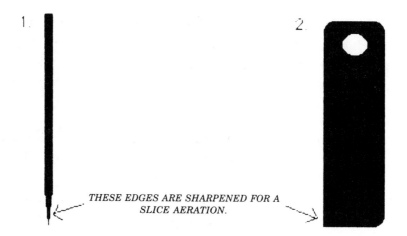

THESE EDGES ARE SHARPENED FOR A
SLICE AERATION.

Drawing 1 is a side view of a power rake key and drawing 2 is a straight-on view. These drawings are very close to actual size and thickness.

The direction of movement, however, is not the same. The keys of a power rake move in a circular straight line; the mower moves in a single rotary direction and the effects upon a lawn are entirely different. Also, the keys on a real power rake are very flexible and giving. But the lawn mower addition is not, and real damage to your lawn's root system can result. I do not recommend using this type of mower attachment. In fact, I have seen many incidents of lawn destruction caused by the use of this product.

BENEFITS OF POWER RAKING

Cut grass, dead leaves, and other plant matter all come together and form loam, which enriches soil. Loam should not be confused with what we call thatch. Grass blades separated or cut from the colony plants are always absorbed back into the soil/loam layer. But stolons and grass blades that have served their purpose and have died off but are still attached to the grass colony (much like hair on humans) do not get absorbed back into soil, and these are what make up the thatch layer. Grass produces thatch as a layer to protect its roots from deadly exposure to elements such as direct sunlight, wind, and people or animals walking across it. This layer also keeps water that seeps in under it from evaporating quickly and letting a lawn dry out.

The problem is that because man has mutated the different strains for his own purposes, grass does not know when to stop producing thatch. With too much thatch a lawn can become yellow and the blades unhealthy due to lack of oxygen, water, and other nutrients unable to penetrate this thick layer.

When thatch reaches a thickness of 1 to 1½ inches, it should be raked out. Using a power rake is the simplest and most effective way to do this. Following is a list of the benefits of correctly applied power raking.

1. *Removal of thatch.* Removing two-thirds of the thatch allows water and fertilizer to more easily reach the roots without running off or evaporating.

2. *New lawn growth.* Lawns without choking thatch are able to send up more new shoots, thus staying renewed, young, and green.

3. *Rough surfaces leveled.* When worms rise to the surface they tend to make hundreds of lumps all over a lawn. The rapid action of power rake keys

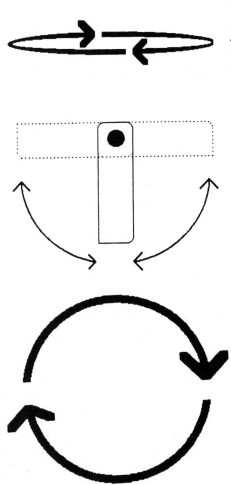

The rotary lawn mower with a "rake" attachment moves in a flat circle, allowing grass to be torn up in the whole circumference of the circle.

Power-rake keys can move back and forth on the retainer, which allows for give-and-take in the action. This prevents damage to the lawn.

A power rake moves in the same fashion as an old-style reel lawn mower. This allows the lawn to be hit only by the keys at the very bottom of the circle.

will reduce these lumps and other surface irregularities by up to 60 percent. There is a note of caution here. Unless the thatch is thick enough to absorb the action, trying to level the unevenness of a lawn will cause more damage than benefit.

WHEN SHOULD YOU POWER RAKE AND HOW OFTEN?

Generally, like aeration, people assume that the best time to power rake a lawn is in the spring. This is not necessarily the case. Most lawns can be raked at any time during the year. In the absence of snow, winter is an acceptable time to power rake, as long as the lawn is dry. And the *middle* of the growing season is an extremely beneficial time. Just be certain in the warmer seasons, that you water more thoroughly in the weeks following the power rake job to help the lawn recover.

Frequency is a different matter. Unless a lawn is growing green and long with plenty of fertilizer and water during the entire growing season, it should not be power raked more than once every three to five years, with the exception of Bermuda grass which *must* be power raked every other year for optimum growth.

A competent professional should decide whether power raking is necessary after examining the lawn.

WHEN IS POWER RAKING INDICATED?

I have heard people talk about how a power rake job has ruined their lawn. On my side, however, I have seen hundreds of lawns that became more green and lush than they had been in years after a correct rake job was performed. Deciding on a power rake for a lawn is like a person deciding on a hair cut for their head. If you try to give someone who is bald a deep and heavy hair cut, not only will the effort be wasted but a lot of damage to the scalp can result. Obviously, you only give haircuts to people who need them; likewise you *only* perform a power rake job on a lawn that requires it. Perform a rake job only when the following severe conditions are present.

When a Lawn Is Yellow Instead of Green

At times the general underlying layer of grass is so thick that the dead yellow color shows more than the green, growing grass does. Removal of two-thirds of the thatch allows less of the dead yellow to show and leaves new space for young green grass shoots to grow in their place.

When Lawn Thatch Base is 1 to 1½ Inches Deep

When thatch is one inch or more, a lawn cannot reach peak growth, thickness, and appearance. A power rake will remove the unneeded two-thirds of the thatch and allow peak growth.

Contraindications

Do not power rake if you have

1. thin grass growing in shade;
2. patchy lawns growing in clumps;
3. grass with less than 1 inch of thatch.

Lawns in these three conditions will only be torn up and damaged by the power rake and no benefit will be derived.

Remember:

Dry ground = best power rake.

Power raking can be done at any time during the year if done correctly. If a rake is done during the intense heat of summer, your lawn should be watered more heavily than normal for one week to prevent burned dry spots. The thatch removed is excellent for garden mulch.

CHAPTER
10

Weeds and Weeding

With the closing of the twentieth century, the general perspective on weeds has undergone a drastic shift. Rather than viewing weeds as highly frustrating enemies that must be fought and destroyed, the new and more correct view is to understand that a weed is just a plant that is growing where someone doesn't want it to. In previous decades, when a so-called weed appeared, it was time to begin applying chemicals in great floods and clouds until the blasted things were dead, gone, and buried. Certainly, chemicals work, and in many cases they are the most efficient means of eradication available. But even after weeds are chemically burned out of a lawn, the fact is, the weeds come back. This means more spraying, more noxious fumes and more threat to a water table that is becoming increasingly contaminated.

It turns out that many of the most effective weed killers have harmful long-term side effects on animals, soil, and even the health of humans. Thus, though weed killers do work as designed, the harm is even more frequently seen as outweighing the benefit.

How damaging are chemical pesticides? Each square meter of healthy topsoil is home to as many as a million organisms, which maintain drainage, fertility, and aeration of the land. A heavy dependence on pesticides and herbicides damages and kills these naturally occurring organisms and interrupts the cycle of decay and absorption that is essential to the survival of plants. Continued use of chemicals will also cause an eventual disruption of the soil's ability to regenerate itself. If this occurs, pests, weeds, and diseases will forge an even greater presence in the affected area.

Even more sobering are the results of studies that show chemicals to have hazardous effects on the health of people who use them on a regular basis. Farmers suffer from a high incidence of deadly diseases, including leukemia and cancers of the liver, prostate, stomach, skin, brain, and lip. Though some of these illnesses can be attributed to continued exposure to radiation in the form of sunlight, many of them have been linked to chemical usage.

It is important to remember that all lawns have an infiltrating weed or two, whether chemicals are used or not. The trick is to keep the numbers low enough to prevent significant damage to the grass. Inversely, healthy grass keeps weeds from taking over.

The first alternative to chemical weed control that is recommended in nearly every article on lawn care is to have the best kept lawn possible. Lawns that are watered correctly, for instance, do not weaken and allow weeds to take over. There are a number of ways to maintain a naturally weed-free lawn.

FIVE NATURAL WEED PREVENTION SOLUTIONS

SOLUTION ONE: Regular Aeration. A major cause of weed problems in lawns is compaction of surface soils. Compacted soil squeezes the life out of the roots of lawn grass, allowing weeds to move in and take control. Fortunately, you can remedy soil compaction by aerating the soil as part of your regular maintenance program, using the machines that remove narrow plugs of sod. The procedure allows oxygen to penetrate the soil, and restores proper drainage and root growth.

Most lawns should be aerated three times a year—in fall, spring, and winter.

SOLUTION TWO: Power Raking (de-thatching). Thatch is a dense layer of dead roots, stems, and stolons that, because they are still attached to the living plant core, are resistant to decay. A deep layer of thatch tends to prevent water and fertilizer from soaking to the soil layer beneath. A thatch layer up to ⅔ inch is acceptable. A thicker layer encourages insects and diseases to propagate, which will in turn create an unhealthy lawn that will allow expanded weed growth.

SOLUTION THREE: Regularly Fertilize. Fertilizing feeds a lawn, revitalizes soil that has been burnt out, and maintains strong root growth. Other than as previously recommended, only use large amounts of fertilizer in the fall or spring. During the rest of the year, apply small amounts on a regular basis.

SOLUTION FOUR: Watering. Improper watering can cause a major influx of weed growth. In most cases, frequent shallow watering promotes shallow root growth, which uses less area of the available surface soil, thus allowing weeds to germinate and grow. If puddles appear on your lawn, aerate and de-thatch. If sod is uneven, level it with topsoil to reduce waterlogged low spots that promote weed growth. Water less at the bottom of a hill and more at the top.

SOLUTION FIVE: Mowing. Astonishingly enough, improper mowing accounts for much of the damage that allows weeds to get a foot hold. Most lawns are mowed too short. If close mowing is combined with other stresses such as drought, insufficient nutrients, or unusually hot or cold spells, grass colonies become smaller in size and less dense. Smaller, thinner grass colonies allow for greater weed growth.

Continual cutting also creates wounds at the ends of grass blades, providing ports of entry for diseases such as leaf spot, rust, and dollar spot. In fact, at the U.S. Department of Agriculture's experimental lawn plots, it is standard practice to mow shorter and more often to incite lawn diseases for experimental use.

Keep your mower blades sharp and as high off the ground as possible. In order to avoid compaction of the soil by the mower wheels, change your mowing patterns frequently.

But when weeds are introduced by wind, lawn equipment, or animal leavings and begin to spread so that you can no longer dig them out by hand, it is best to seek professional advice on the best method of removal.

Though this chapter lists many types of weeds in an effort to help with positive identification, chemical remedies can change frequently. Detailed and current advice on the latest weed controls is best obtained from nursery or garden supply center experts.

WEED CATEGORIES

Weeds are categorized according to several traits. First, they are either perennials or annuals. Perennials are those that live for two or more years. Annual weeds are those that live only one year. Weeds are further categorized by their leaf types—broad-leaved or narrow-leaved. Those that are broad-leaved have easily observed flowers and their leaves have a pattern of small veins that sometimes divide the leaves in half; an example is thistle. The narrow-leaved variety includes grasses, which have hollow stems and long, narrow leaf blades with parallel veins. Another, much less common weed group is sedges. They look like grasses but have triangular stems.

COMMON WEEDS TO WATCH FOR

Clover (annual, broad-leaved) has several different varieties. White clover and Burclover are the problem in most lawns. Clover forms thick patches that

Clover has many varieties. White clover is the problem variety—this weed forms thick patches that choke out grass.

choke out grass and create an uneven appearance in an otherwise smooth lawn.

Crabgrass (annual, narrow-leaved) is noted for its broad blades and rough texture. Crabgrass begins in early spring and grows fast until the seed head forms in summer or early fall.

Dandelion (perennial, broad-leaved) has a bright yellow flower that soon brings a halo of seeds to scatter in the wind. This weed sends down a root sometimes as far as a foot and a half, and if only two inches of the root survives a removal, it is enough for the plant to continue to grow. It grows best in spring and fall.

Dock (perennial, broad-leaved) looks similar to dandelion, but the leaves are less green and glossy and have a "twisted" appearance.

Crabgrass has broad blades and is rough textured. It is sometimes called "Orchard grass."

Dandelions spread fast and easily. To get rid of a plant the entire root must be eliminated.

Ground Ivy (perennial, broad-leaved) has leaves that are rounded like a kidney and tube-shaped flowers that are purple or blue. This trailing plant has creeping stems that form thick masses wherever they get a foothold.

Henbit (annual, broad-leaved) has a four-sided stem and is a variety of the mint family. It grows best during the spring and fall.

Knotweed (annual, broad-leaved) grows particularly in hard, compacted soils. Aeration will help eliminate it as a problem. It thrives from early spring through early fall.

Mallow (annual, broad-leaved), often called cheeseweed, gets started in early spring and has a long growing season.

Ground Ivy has leaves that are shaped like a kidney. This trailing plant has creeping stems that form thick masses.

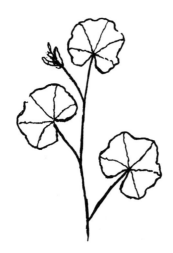

Mallow grows from several stems, but has one deep—and very difficult to remove—main root. This plant is sometimes called "cheeseweed."

Mouse-Ear Chickweed (perennial, broad-leaved) has very small leaves that are dark green. It grows fast and plentiful in the cool weather of spring and fall.

Oxalis (perennial, broad-leaved) grows best in spring and late fall. It looks similar to clover and henbit, but its leaves are more fragile and a lighter green.

Plantain (perennial, broad-leaved) comprises a group of low-growing herbs, several of which are common weeds that invade lawns. They have a circular cluster of bright green leaves that grow directly from the roots. Tall, slender spikes sprout from the center of the cluster.

Purslane (annual, broad-leaved) looks similar to spurge but has thicker leaves that are glossy in appearance and rubbery in texture. It grows all summer long.

Plantains have fleshy leaves sent up from one root system and stem. Seed stems must not be allowed to grow.

Purslane has glossy green leaves with one stem and many branches.

Spurge (annual, broad-leaved) has small inconspicuous flowers called *bracts,* leaves that look like flower petals, and a biting milky juice. There are 7,300 species in this family of herbs, including some shrubs and trees. Spurge grows fastest in late spring and early fall.

Thistle (perennial, broad-leaved) comprises a group of plants that have sharp spines or prickles. The two North American varieties are *tall thistle* and *pasture thistle.* Tough fibrous stems, prickly leaves with many lobes, and soft, silky flowers that are usually purple or pinkish characterize these plants.

Tree Saplings Certain trees propagate by sending out roots—sometimes up to a hundred feet—that push up shoots to form saplings. A good example is

Spotted spurge has one main root growing straight down, yet the plant itself sends out long branches with many tiny leaves.

Thistles are characterized by tough, fibrous stems, prickly leaves, and purple or pinkish flowers.

the mountain west poplar variety called *Quaking Aspen*. When a tree of this kind borders a lawn, the saplings can be quite bothersome. And if they are just cut off every week with a mower, a hard knot or blister of wood forms.

Veronica (annual, broad-leaved), also called speedwell, is very low lying, has tiny light blue flowers and tiny green leaves, and is very tough to kill. There are several barely varying species. Seed pods are heart-shaped. It grows best in spring and fall.

NOTE: Many weeds simply do not do enough damage to a lawn to warrant wholesale efforts at complete and utter eradication. Dandelions, however, can quickly take over and damage even a healthy lawn. Fortunately, dandelions are easy to control with the use of any product that contains 2,4-D. This compound is my favorite to use when there is no other choice but to go with a chemical. 2,4-D is not a sterilizer, but instead hyperstimulates a plant so that it will out-grow itself to death. Another weed that does a lot of damage to a lawn is crabgrass. Crabgrass is also considered to be a very tough weed to eliminate. But I have SUCCESSFULLY eliminated it over and over again simply by applying proper lawn growth and maintenance techniques.

MORE ON WEED CONTROL

There are four general methods of weed control—*cultural, mechanical, biological*, and *chemical*.

Cultural control is the use of efficient lawn variety to prevent weeds from growing. Also included is the technique of planting grass in an area that has been made weed free by the use of a mulch, grass clippings, or plastic sheeting.

Mechanical control is the destruction of weeds manually or by a machine. Many weeds can be removed by hand; these are weeds with shallower root systems. Others can be removed with the help of tools that can reach down deep and remove a long root entirely. Sometimes a specific technique of mowing will kill a weed in a lawn.

Biological control involves the use of natural enemies of weeds growing in a specific area. For example, insects and other small animals that eat certain weeds may be introduced into a lawn where those weeds are growing. Bacteria and other organisms can be used to spread diseases among specific species of weeds. Sometimes a certain amount of watering is an enemy to a weed, depending on the area and species of the weed.

Chemical control is the use of chemical compounds called herbicides. Most herbicides are selective—that is, they kill weeds but do not harm the grass, human beings, or wildlife.

Many herbicides, however, are not selective. They can only be sprayed directly on the plant and must not be touched by humans or animals for a specified amount of time. These non-selectives seem to be the most effective means of removing troublesome weeds; however, they must be painstakingly applied to each individual weed.

Following is a list of herbicides that can be applied to rid weeds from a patch of ground *before* planting.

Atrazine controls several annual grasses and broad-leaved weeds, but only in lawns of centipede grass, St. Augustine grass, or zoysia grass. It does not harm woody ornamental plants.

Benefin will control annual grasses in many lawns, but is not safe for bent grasses. It prevents all seeds from germinating for about eight weeks.

Bensulide is a control for annual grasses and certain broad-leaved weeds. Seeds will not grow for four months after an application. It is safe for use on bent-grass lawns.

DCPA is especially deadly to germinating seeds of certain broad-leaved species, including chickweed and purslane. This is damaging to new lawns, and reseeding cannot be done for eleven to thirteen weeks. It is not recommended for bent grass.

Oxadiazon controls annual grasses. Do not use on fine fescue or bent grass. Do not reseed for at least four months.

Pendimethalin is used for many annual grasses and some broad-leaved weeds. It is not recommended for bent grass.

Siduron works well on weedy grasses, including crabgrass, foxtail, and barnyard grass. Siduron has the unique trait of not interfering with the germination of cool season grasses such as Kentucky bluegrass.

Following is a list of herbicides that are applied *after* planting:

CAMA, MAMA, MSMA are a group of chemicals called organic arsenicals. They control grassy weeds like crabgrass and foxtail, and are effective against some nutsedges. More than one application is required.

Cacodylic acid kills only on contact. Repeat treatments are needed to kill hardy perennials. This chemical works by killing all green growing leaf tissue. It will not move through a plant to the root system. It is also sometimes used to clear weeds from an area prior to planting a lawn.

Dalapon is used against all grasses. Spot treatment is the most efficient and effective method of application. Residual toxicity can last for four months.

Dicamba is frequently used against clover, chickweed, and knotweed. Dicamba affects plant hormones. It is absorbed through the roots and leaves. Do not use where roots of desirable plants may run under the area to be treated.

Glyphosate is nonselective and systemic, meaning it kills both grasses *and* broad-leaved weeds. It is an effective chemical for most perennial grassy weeds.

MCPP is similar to 2,4-D but is safe to use on new lawns or sensitive grasses such as bent grass or St. Augustine grass.

2,4-D is available in many forms. It is a growth-influencing hormone that affects broad-leaved weeds in a lawn and kills them. This herbicide works with little damage to most existing lawns.

2,4-DP is very similar to 2,4-D. It controls hard-to-kill broad-leaved weeds. Some examples are oxalis and mugwort.

Remember: New weed controls are constantly being developed and old ones eliminated. Keep in touch with your local garden supply dealer for the most up-to-date advice.

CHAPTER
11

Lawn Diseases

O n planet Earth, everyone and everything is subject to depredations and attack by diseases of one sort or another. Lawn grass colonies are no exception to this rule. Yet, the cause of lawn disease can always be directly attributed to one deficiency or another in your lawn's ecosystem. Thus, as with appropriate weed prevention, the best form of disease prevention and eradication is proper lawn care.

The appearance of a disease in a lawn is like a barometer, telling any gardener who is listening and watching that a problem is developing in some aspect of the property medium. If you listen to what the disease is telling you, you can address the underlying cause before other afflictions such as weeds and insects move in to take advantage of the existing deficiency. Possible sources of lawn deficiencies include high levels of thatch, excessive moisture, improper watering procedures and times, mowing with a dull blade, poor drainage, water pooling (because of compacted soil or poor irrigation), drought, and improper fertilizing techniques. By addressing and/or avoiding these problems, you can usually avert the problems associated with lawn diseases. The following are a few things to keep in mind when it comes to preventing lawn diseases.

MOWING: Mowing your lawn either too low or with a dull blade can cause unnecessary stress to your grass, thereby increasing your chances of developing a lawn disease. Always make sure you are mowing your grass within recommended mowing height and that you are keeping your mower blade sharp for a better cut. In addition, if you already have a lawn disease, make sure that when mowing you bag your clippings and thoroughly wash down your mower after you are done. Lawn diseases can spread through clippings that cling to mower blades and even to your shoes. Make sure that you are not helping diseases to spread.

WATERING AND DRAINAGE: Since most disease fungi love water and moisture, you may be providing an hospitable disease environment if your lawn does not drain well. If you commonly have water "pooling", or heavy levels of water run-off in your yard, then you could develop disease troubles in these areas. If you have these problems, make sure you either adjust your drainage away from your home, and/or even re-grade your lawn for better run-off. Additionally, watering your lawn during late evenings in certain regions can lead to disease problems. Make sure that you water in the early morning hours so that your lawn has enough time to soak up the water and have a dry surface before nightfall.

THATCH: Excess thatch buildup in your lawn can help trap moisture in it, increasing the likelihood of disease development. If you are fertilizing often and if your grass is growing well and strong because of perfect growing conditions, you will eventually have a thatch base buildup. Make sure that you have your lawn properly aerated several times a year and have it de-thatched whenever the need arises to help prevent a moisture accumulation in the root area of your lawn.

FERTILIZING: Some lawn diseases thrive on lawns that receive too much nitrogen during fertilization. This causes excessive top-growth which can be susceptible to disease. Make sure you properly fertilize your lawn by using fertilizing tables and adjusting them according to your specific grass type and local climate. As an additional precaution, when fertilizing (usually in the fall), you can use fertilizer with a fungus control.

It can be extremely difficult to diagnose a problem because many of the characteristics of lawn disease are similar to other problems, such as tree roots under a lawn or a poor watering program. Then again, one of these conditions may be the direct cause of a recurring disease.

If prevention measures are applied religiously and a serious disease still takes hold, chemical control may be necessary. Most diseases can be controlled with the use of chemicals, but some, such as stripe smut fungus, can be controlled only by planting disease-resistant grass. Consult a professional for analysis and identification of the disease before resorting to extreme measures for removal.

SOME COMMON DISEASES

Brown Patch

Description: Large, irregular, circular areas up to several feet in diameter. The spots are usually brown to gray in color and have a water-soaked appearance around the edges. These signs are usually only seen on leaves and stems.

Brown patch is shown here as it affects a large surface. The appearance is similar to that of fertilizer burn.

Most affected grasses: Centipede grass, St. Augustine grass, Bermuda grass, bent grass, ryegrass, and zoysia grass.

Cultural control: Do not overdose with nitrogen. Aerate and water deeply. Remove sources of excess shade. Power rake whenever minimum need arises.

Chemical control: Use anilazine, benomyl, chlorothalonil, fenarimol, thiophanates, or triadmimefon.

Cottony Blight

Description: This disease is sometimes called grease spot blight. It can affect an area of a few inches or several feet in diameter. The diseased area will be surrounded by blackened blades covered with a white or gray mildew. Dry weather will halt the disease.

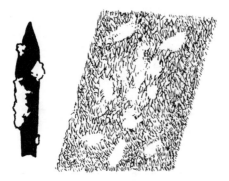

Typhula blight grows on individual blades of grass in this form and causes a damage pattern to an entire area.

Most affected grasses: bent grass, Bermuda grass, ryegrass, and fescues.

Cultural control: Aerate profusely. Avoid watering heavily. Do not use excessive fertilizer.

Chemical control: Apply fungicides like propamocarb, etridiazole, chloroneb, or metalyaxyl.

Dollar Spot

Description: A fungus that attacks several different varieties of grass, it kills in small spots that are 3 to 12 inches in diameter. Many spots can, however, come together to form a large dead area. Affected areas usually range in color from dark tan to light yellow.

Most affected grasses: Bermuda grass, all fescues, Kentucky bluegrass, and ryegrass.

Cultural control: Use larger amounts of nitrogen. Aerate and water for longer periods. Decrease thatch through hand or mechanical means.

Chemical control: Use anilazine, benomyl, chlorothalonil, fenarimol, iprodione, thiophanates, triadimefon.

Dollar spot affects grass blades in this pattern.

Fairy Rings

Description: Indicated by rings or arcs of dark green, fast-growing grass from several inches to over 40 feet. Fairy rings expand outward at a rate of anywhere from 2 inches to 4 feet per year. Rings may spring up as a result of buried organic matter such as lumber, logs, roots, or stumps, and are produced by any one of over fifty different kinds of fungus.

Lawns beautify any location—be it home, office, or park. In hot weather, grass will actually cool the air near the Earth's surface, acting as a super-efficient, natural air-conditioner. Lawns even reduce noise pollution by absorbing sound.

Grasses help to prevent soil erosion.

A good ground cover is an excellent alternative for locations that cannot support grass growth, such as shady or rocky areas.

Much of the success in planting a lawn depends on how well the soil is prepared beforehand. Unlike a vegetable or flower garden, where the soil can be changed and built up each fall and spring, a lawn grows in the same soil year after year.

When grading a lawn, avoid any steep slopes—gentle and smooth slopes are prettier and easier to maintain. A one-to one-and-a-half-foot drop in ten linear feet is excellent.

The yard should be graded so that it slopes away from the house to carry off surplus water.

There are grasses for damp areas, shade, and direct sunlight. Examine your property and pick out the seed or turf that will grow best in each section. Do not be afraid to have different varieties of grass in different areas of your yard.

The ground should be deeply watered for a week before laying sod. Lay the sod in a bricklayer's pattern, making sure that the slanted edges are matched to fit evenly.

Overseeding—scattering a different variety of grass seed throughout an existing lawn— is a great way to change the appearance of an ailing lawn. As long as the seed is planted and scattered uniformly, the new grass will eventually blend perfectly with the old.

A well-defined border and neatly trimmed edge can make an otherwise average lawn the envy of the neighborhood.

Perfectly edged lawn.

Badly edged lawn.

A power edger is the best tool for creating edges where none existed before.

A hand-held bladed edger may be used to maintain the edges once they have been established.

Many homeowners make the mistake of using a weed eater to reestablish a neglected edge or maintain edges along walks and drives. This results in a butchered, rounded edge.

Electric lawn mowers do not contribute directly to air pollution, are quiet, and are mechanically very reliable. Now there are battery-operated mowers that are charged overnight and can mow an average size lawn on a single charge.

Many people prefer rear baggers because of the convenience of not having to maneuver a machine with a bag sticking out to the side.

Side baggers are generally less expensive than rear baggers. They require minimal care and maintenance, and breakdowns are few and far between.

Riding lawn mowers are impractical for any but the largest lawns. They have a large turning radius and are too large to fit through most gates or paths connecting front- and backyards.

For the first two or three cuttings of the season, the lawn mower should be set at one inch. After that, as the weather gets hotter, the blade should be raised to anywhere from one and a half to two inches, depending on climate, variety of grass, and personal preference. With most varieties of grass, the higher you can stand to cut, the healthier the lawn will look.

Cutting the grass too short results in lawn mower burn.

As a mower rolls over a lawn, its tires lightly crush and bend the blades of grass to create a pattern. Cutting patterns can be arranged in attractive designs such as the simple square cut and diamond cut.

Trenching machines are used to install sprinkler systems.

PVC pipe is used today almost exclusively in the construction of sprinkler systems. It's easy to install and seal against leaking and does not rust.

Drip-style sprinkler systems feed water directly to the roots without exposure to the sun or air. There is little or no evaporation, which saves water and money.

Pop-up half head sprinkler.

Pop-up quarter-round sprinkler.

Multistream sprinkler head.

Nothing helps a lawn maintain peak condition like regular aeration. For maximum benefit a lawn should be aerated three times a year. It is best to rent a hollow spike aerator or to have a professional do it. The benefits of aeration include better root growth, less water evaporation, increased watershed, and the elimination of fungus problems.

Aeration plugs on a lawn.

A hollow spike aerator.

Grass does not generally grow well under trees where it has to compete for sunlight and nutrients.

For shady areas, such as underneath trees, it's a good idea to construct small gardens of shade-tolerant plants.

Shallow watering will produce shallow rooting as tree roots seek water at the surface.

A weed is just a plant that is growing where someone doesn't want it to. It is important to remember that all lawns have an infiltrating weed or two, whether chemicals are used or not. The trick is to keep the numbers low enough to prevent significant damage to the grass. Inversely, by keeping your lawn healthy, it is possible to prevent weeds naturally from taking over.

Mallow, a broad-leaved annual, is often called cheeseweed. It gets started in early spring and has a long growing season.

Thistle refers to a group of broad-leaved perennials with sharp spines or prickles. The two North American varieties are tall thistle and pasture thistle. Tough fibrous stems, prickly leaves with many lobes, and soft, silky flowers that are usually purple or pinkish characterize these plants.

The dandelion, a broad-leaved perennial, sends down a root sometimes as far as a foot and a half and if only 2 inches of the root survives a removal, it is enough for the plant to continue to grow.

Plantains comprise a group of low-growing herbs, several of which are weeds that commonly invade lawns. They have a circular cluster of bright green leaves that grow directly from the roots. Tall, slender spikes grow up from the center of the cluster.

Sod webworms live in the grass root system but surface to devour leaves and stems with an unstoppable hunger. Dead patches from one to two inches in diameter appear in the midst of otherwise healthy grass. Many birds feeding regularly on the lawn can indicate a high concentration of this insect. Sod worms can be discovered by examining a few two-inch clods of grass taken from an area of suspected infestation.

Cutworms are extremely difficult to spot, not only because they live deep in the root system, but also because the damage they cause looks like so many other diseases and ailments. Cutworms eat the tender roots of the plant, which causes dead brown spots to form in round and irregular patches. A telltale sign of cutworms is that the brown and dying grass will pull free with no attachment to the roots.

Lawn disease can always be attributed to one deficiency or another in your lawn's eco-system. Thus, the best disease prevention and eradication is proper lawn care. The appearance of a disease in a lawn is like a barometer, telling any gardener who is listening and watching that a problem is developing in some aspect of the property medium.

Fusarium blight, commonly known as summer patch, first manifests itself in light green patches one-half inch to eight inches in diameter. These turn tan or reddish brown. When the patches are large, a "frog eye" pattern occurs with apparently healthy patches of grass partially surrounded by rings of dead grass.

There are ailments that appear to be caused by disease but in fact are due to deficiencies in lawn care. This lawn, for example, needs fertilizer. The green clumps indicate places where dog droppings have greened the lawn. If all of the lawn were fertilized properly, it would be as green as the clumps.

Xeriscapes require little or no weeding or watering—a great benefit in dry climates where water is a precious commodity. But these dry rocky landscapes are little comfort to those who still love a soft, green, lawn.

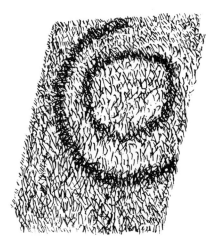

Fairy rings are usually caused by organic matter under the surface of a lawn. There can be a single such ring, or up to three or more.

Most affected grasses: all grasses.

Cultural control: Apply increased nitrogen to hide the problem. Aerate profusely. Keep area wet for about two weeks and mow frequently. If this does not work, replace the soil to a depth of twelve inches or more and sod.

Chemical control: There are no easy-to-use or entirely adequate chemicals to recommend at the time of this writing.

Fusarium Patch

Description: Sometimes called pink snow mold, this disease most often develops under snow but can occur when no snow is present. Can be identified by white or pink circular patches that are one to eight inches in diameter.

Most affected grasses: Kentucky bluegrass, creeping bent grass, ryegrass, and zoysia grass.

Cultural control: Decrease amount of shade in the affected area. Aerate well. Avoid any thatch buildup. Do not overfertilize.

Chemical control: Use applications of benomyl, fenarimol, mancozeb, or tradimefon.

Leaf Spots

Description: Indicated by purplish-black, dark reddish brown, chocolate brown, light gray, or tan spots on leaves and stems. The spots can be round or oblong and may cause entire colonies of grass to turn yellow. Turf becomes thin, weak, or dies out in round or irregular spots that enlarge during summer months.

Most affected grasses: Delta, Kenblue, and Park Kentucky bluegrass.

Cultural control: Reduce the amount of shade. Improve aeration for better water drainage. Mow at top limit of cutting height.

Gray leaf spot affects blades in this pattern.

Chemical control: Apply anilazine, mancozeb, captan, iprodione, chloro-thalonil, or cycloheximide.

Mosses

Description: These occur in lawns that are low in nutrients and fertility with poor drainage, high acidity, too much shade, improper watering, or a combi-nation of these. They appear as light green to dark green, fuzzy or slimy growths that cover soil, grass, or objects such as rocks and garden ornaments.

Most affected grasses: All grasses where the above-mentioned conditions predominate.

Cultural control: Aerate well, rake affected area, remove causes of excess shade, use fertilizer such as ammonium sulfate.

Chemical control: Use maneb, mancozeb, or wettable sulfur. These solutions are only temporary. Cultural control to eliminate the cause is the only perma-nent solution.

Powdery Mildew

Description: These mildews grow when nights are cool and days are warm. They occur mostly on bluegrasses and fescues. The mildew color is white, gray-white, and brown. Patches can be seen on leaves in shaded or poorly drained areas. The leaves can yellow and wither. This is most serious on new plantings.

Most affected grasses: Bermuda grass, Kentucky bluegrass, and zoysia grass.

Cultural control: Remove causes of excess shade. Do not overwater and frequently aerate well. Do not overfertilize.

Chemical control: Benomyl, cycloheximide, or triadimefon.

Red Thread

Description: Sometimes this disease is called Pink Patch. It affects mostly fescues, bent, and bluegrasses. Irregularly shaped pink patches of dead grass two to six inches or more in diameter develop during cool, damp weather in spring, fall, and winter. Usually only leaves are affected. If the disease is very severe, patches turn brown and the leaves die. Characteristic: coral-pink threads bind leaves together.

Most affected grasses: Kentucky bluegrass, red fescue, and ryegrass.

Cultural control: Use more nitrogen.

Chemical control: Anilazine, chlorothalonil, iprodione, mancozeb, or triadimefon.

Rust

Description: This problem is indicated by orange, reddish-brown, yellow, or black powdery deposits on leaves and leaf sheaths. If severe, leaves may yellow, wither, and die. Grass may be thinned, weakened, and more susceptible to drought, winter injury, and other diseases.

Most affected grasses: Kentucky bluegrass and ryegrass. All commonly grown grasses are susceptible.

Chemical control: Apply anilazine, chlorothalonil, cycloheximide, maneb, or triadimefon.

Slime Molds

Description: These occur in warm weather following heavy watering or rains. Small white, gray, or yellow slimy masses grow up and over grass surfaces in round to irregular patches, shading or discoloring otherwise healthy turf. Masses dry to form bluish, gray, yellow, black, or white powdery growths.

Most affected grasses: common Kentucky bluegrass, zoysia grass, bent grass, and fescue.

Cultural control: Aerate thoroughly. De-thatch even if thatch layer is less than one-third inch. Cut grass to lowest limit of height for your recommended variety.

Chemical control: Use benomyl, fenarimol, or triadimefon.

Stripe Smut

Description: Long or short stripes in leaves that rupture and release dark brown or black powdery masses. Sometimes leaves are shredded, wilted, and withered. Grass can yellow and later die in patches two to eight inches in diameter.

Most affected grasses: bent grass and Kentucky bluegrass.

Cultural control: Do not over water. Aerate regularly and keep thatch to a minimum.

Chemical control: Use PCNB, thiophanates, or triadimefon.

Summer Patch

Description: Sometimes called fusarium blight, summer patch starts out as light green patches that are ½ inch to 8 inches in diameter. These turn tan or reddish brown. When the patches are large, a characteristic called "frog eye"

Stripe smut can take over large areas of a lawn. Long black stripes are seen on ruptured blades.

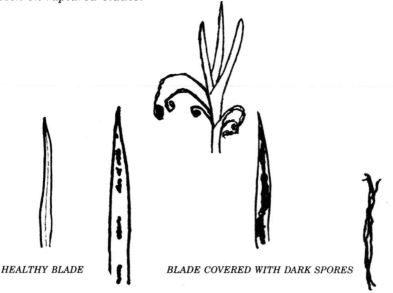

HEALTHY BLADE   BLADE COVERED WITH DARK SPORES

BEGINNING SMUT PATCHES   BLADE SHRIVELS AND DIES

occurs. This is where a healthy-appearing patch of grass is partially surrounded by a ring of dead grass.

Most affected grasses: Kentucky bluegrass, perennial ryegrass, and tall fescues.

Cultural control: Frequent light watering helps during drought. Mow in medium range of height recommended for your grass variety.

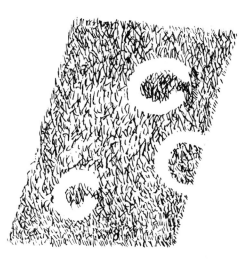

Here summer patch disease is shown in the frog-eye pattern. The affected areas are usually brown or dull tan.

Chemical control: Benomyl, iprodione, thiophanates, fenarimol, or triadimefon.

All in all, there are more than twenty-one lawn disease groups that include more than a hundred different ailments. Also, some individual diseases are known by different names in different areas, making reference to each and every disease or ailment impossible in this work.

Using the above-mentioned general descriptions, however, you can get a closer idea of which ailment could be affecting your lawn and thus take appropriate measures. As in all lawn problems, the advice of a professional has no substitute.

DAMAGE CAUSED BY NEGLECT

At times there are ailments that appear to be caused by disease but in fact are due to deficiencies in lawn care. It is important to be able to recognize these first, since they are relatively easy to remedy.

Chemical Burn

Description: Lawns damaged by dog defecation, spilled or over applied fertilizer or herbicides, or gasoline, are characterized by round to irregular patches of dead yellow grass that will eventually (if not treated) blow and wash away to leave patches of bare soil.

Treatment: In the case of dog defecation and fertilizer burn, completely soak the soil with water. New seeds or grass sod replacements will be necessary for a quick cure.

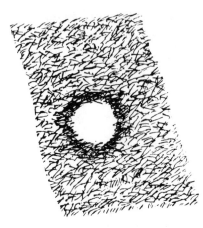

Fertilizer burn and dog-defecation problems appear very similar. The edges of the dead areas will be very green and seem more healthy than the normal grass because of the abundance of food.

Chemical burn creates a dead area. The spots look similar to a fertilizer burn but the edges will not be green.

In the case of gasoline or herbicide burn, soak the damaged area with soapy water that is about the consistency of dishwater. Then rinse completely with plain water. These bare patches will fill in in one to three months. The only quick cure is still seeding or sodding.

Dull Mower and Scalping

Description: Cutting your lawn with a dull blade gives it a grayish cast one or two days after it is mowed. This occurs because the grass is shredded instead of being cleanly cut. Then the shreds turn brown. Shredded tips allow easy entry for many diseases.

Scalping occurs when too much lawn (more than one-third reduction in height) is cut off at one time. The lawn will turn brown and sparse. This should not be mistaken for disease damage.

Treatment: The cures for these problems are simple and logical. Raise the height of your mower blade a half inch or more from the present height to prevent scalping, and buy a new blade or sharpen the old one to prevent shredding.

Nitrogen or Iron Deficiency

Description: Grass needs more nitrogen than any other nutrient. If not enough nitrogen has been applied, your lawn will be yellowish and will not grow very well. If nitrogen is applied and it still does not grow and stays yellow, the problem may be lack of iron.

Treatment: Using a normal fertilizer on a lawn that needs iron will actually cause the grass to become yellower. It is best to apply both nitrogen and iron in tandem—apply them in a fertilizer that contains both.

Summer Dry Spots

Description: Hard, dry soil is a problem with all grasses. This problem occurs most often when the spring has been very wet and then summer heat follows closely behind. The grass becomes used to the continued moisture and only seeks water from the surface. When the heat arrives, the surface water dries up quickly and the lawn develops spots of brown grass, thin yellowish blades, and noticeable areas of soil showing through sparse growths of grass.

Treatment: Institute a watering program. Be certain that all areas of grass are covered and overlapped by any existing sprinkler system. If all areas are not covered sufficiently, a portable hose may be needed to water in dry areas.

LAWN FUNGICIDES

There are two basic types of fungicide: *Systemic,* which gets inside of a plant to kill diseases, and *non-systemic,* which kills disease on the outside of plants. Systemic fungicides work the best, but they are selective, only killing certain diseases. Non-systemic fungicides are usually applied as a preventive measure. Bear in mind that the effective life of these chemicals can be fleeting. New studies are performed all the time in which careful evaluations are made as to whether a given chemical is more harmful to our planetary ecosystem than any benefit derived from it. Do not be surprised if a chemical compound that you have used before or that you want to use in the future is suddenly not available on the market.

Anilazine is non-systemic. It is used against brown patch, typhula blight, rust, dollar spot, leaf spot, and red thread.

Benomyl is systemic. It is used against brown patch, fusarium patch, dollar spot, summer patch and powdery mildew.

Captan is non-systemic. It is used against most leaf spots.

Chloroneb is non-systemic. It is used against pythium blight.

Chlorothalonil is non-systemic. It is used against brown patch, rust, dollar spot, leaf spot, and red thread.

Cycloheximide is non-systemic. It is used against leaf spot, powdery mildew, and rust.

Fenarimol is systemic. It is used against brown patch, typhula blight, fusarium patch, dollar patch, and summer patch.

Iprodione is systemic. It is used against brown patch, summer patch, red thread, typhula blight, dollar patch, and fusarium patch.

Mancozeb is non-systemic. It is used against red thread, leaf spot, and fusarium patch.

Maneb is non-systemic. It is used against rust and some leaf spots.

Metalxyl is systemic. It is used against cottony blight.

PCNB is partially systemic. It is used against stripe smut and some leaf spots.

Propamocarb is systemic. It is used against cottony blight.

Thiophanetes is systemic. It is used against summer patch, brown patch, stripe smut, and dollar spot.

Triadimefon is systemic. It is used against dollar spot, brown patch, red thread, rust, fusarium patch, powdery mildew, stripe smut, summer patch, and typhula blight.

Note: I knew a man who struggled quite unsuccessfully for several years to rid his lawn of a recurring disease. When he finally consulted a professional, who recommended that he eradicate the old lawn completely and plant a new hardy mixture that included vigorous ryegrasses, the problem was at last solved. But what the property owner was most amazed about was the old lawn, even when it had been at its best before the disease, never looked half as beautiful and lush as his new hardy mixture. Do not always assume that a disease is a problem. Often the appearance of disease is only a wakeup call to the real problems; the wrong use specific grass strains, bad soil, etc.

CHAPTER
12

Lawn Pests

Families on camping trips apply mosquito repellant. Homeowners spend Saturday mornings spreading weed-n-feed products on their lawns. A cleaning lady bleaches and disinfects a bathroom. A mother sprinkles a few mothballs into boxes while packing away winter clothing.

What activity do all of these people have in common? They are all using pesticides, though they may not recognize them as such.

WHAT ARE PESTICIDES?

Put simply, pesticides are chemical compounds used to control pests of one sort or another. Examples include insecticides, which control insects; rodenticides, which control rodents; fungicides, to control the spread of fungal diseases of plants; and herbicides, which control weeds and other plants.

WHY ARE PESTICIDES IMPORTANT?

Pesticides control insect pests and thus prevent the diseases they spread on food and fiber crops. Some are used to control parasites on farm animals and pets. Others help maintain human health; e.g., disinfectants are used to cleanse kitchens and bathrooms of parasitical infestations, and repellents ward off ticks and other pests that carry disease. And most important for our purposes here, pesticides can help control infestations of pests in a lawn area.

ARE PESTICIDES NECESSARY?

Sometimes pesticides are necessary, but not in every situation. Many times, non-chemical control methods may be preferable. It is prudent to know and understand as many available options as possible in a given situation in order to reduce pesticide use whenever possible.

PEST MANAGEMENT STRATEGIES

The first step in pest management is to identify the pest that might be causing the problem. Many kinds of insects and pests live in grass and lawns. Some are visible, and some are far too small to be seen. Some are annoying to lawn owners but do little or no actual damage to grass; others can obliterate a once perfectly healthy lawn.

Unfortunately, many of the characteristics of a lawn damaged by insects or pests are identical to those of a lawn damaged by disease or neglect. Diagnosis can therefore be quite difficult. A good pest management strategy incorporates some or all of the methods available to manage a given pest situation. This is called *integrated pest management,* or IPM. The goal should be to reduce pest populations, thus limiting the damage to your lawn to economically and aesthetically tolerable levels. Complete eradication is not always possible, practical, or even desirable.

Judicious selection of pest control methods should be aimed at reducing or eliminating pesticide use whenever possible. This is extremely important because of valid concerns about our personal and environmental safety. The following methods should be considered first when developing a pest management strategy for your lawn.

EXCLUSION

One of the safest and most effective ways to manage pests is to deny them access. This is called exclusion, or pest proofing, and may be accomplished via one of the following options.

Exclusion by Regulation Government embargoes and quarantines are designed to prevent the introduction of pests from one country or locality into another. It's unwise to import live plots of sod from states with a different climate from your own. These sod pieces could introduce a pest to your area that has no naturally existing enemy. If there is a different strain of grass you want to introduce into your property, purchase and import seeds, not sod.

Mechanical Exclusion This includes barriers such as fences to keep out rabbits and noisemakers to ward off ground squirrels. When you are seeding your lawn, you can keep birds away with scarecrows and noisemakers.

CULTURAL CONTROL

Most plants and animals resist pests best when they are in good health. Therefore, keeping a lawn healthy can and will help prevent pest damage.

Grass Selection It is important to use strains and cultivars that are recommended for the rigors of your particular climate. Professionals and databases should be consulted to determine which kinds of grasses grow best with the fewest pest problems.

Sanitation Sanitation is perhaps the most important cultural practice that can be used to help manage pests. It consists of removing grass sections suspected of harboring disease-spreading insects. For instance, a deep thatch layer provides an initial home for many different lawn pests. By removing a major portion of this layer, the breeding ground for these lawn pests can be eliminated. Routine sanitation at the beginning and end of the season includes mowing the grass much shorter than normal.

Mow Properly Improper mowing practices result in more damage to lawns than any other cultural factor. Many lawns are mowed too short, too infrequently, and with a dull blade. This restricts root growth and increases disease, drought, and especially *insect* damage.

Water For Health Not only will a correctly established watering procedure make your lawn strong, green, and beautiful, it will also deter most lawn pests, which do not like living in damp conditions. These pests themselves are susceptible to diseases and parasites that are fostered by too much dampness. Also, eggs left by many of these pests will not hatch unless the soil is dry for an extended period.

One of the best, simplest methods of determining whether suspected insects or pests are present is by simple observation. In many cases, if the damage is extensive enough to be noticed, and the cause is a pest or insect, the organism can be sighted at night or by delving into the soil during the day. The following pages contain descriptions and characteristics of many lawn pests.

TYPES OF PEST DAMAGE

There are three basic categories of insects that damage grass. One is the insect that lives above ground and sucks the plant juice. The second is the kind that lives below the surface and feeds on roots. And the third is the insect that lives at the soil surface and feeds on the grass blades.

The observable symptom of the first category is grass blades thinning out and turning brown. Whole patches of dead and dying grass in round to irregular shapes can appear.

The most noticeable symptom of category two is that blades turn yellow and die in irregularly shaped patches. When a person grabs a handful of grass in these damaged areas, blades will come free and lightly out of the grass without any roots attached.

Category three's symptoms are quite noticeable. Round bare areas can appear, with the grass chewed right down to root level.

LAWN INSECTS

Armyworms chew off the grass blades from below the surface and cause round, bare areas in a lawn. If there are many armyworms present, the grass will be chewed off right to the soil level. Armyworms are yellowish white and have an upside-down Y on their heads.

For chemical control use acephate, diazinon, chlorpyrifos, or carbaryl.

Billbugs feed on grass roots and create small circular patterns of damaged grass that turns yellow and brown. Dead sections of grass will easily lift away from the soil. There are many different species of billbugs that attack different varieties of grass.

For chemical control use diazinon.

Billbugs (here shown in larval stage and adult stage) feed on roots and stems.

Chiggers do not do much damage to a lawn, but they are an extreme nuisance to lawn owners. They are not insects, but are spider mites that lay their eggs in soil. After hatching, the larvae crawl onto grass blades and latch on to any passing person or animal.

For chemical control use diazinon or chlorpyrifos.

Cinch Bugs damage lawns by sucking the juice directly from the leaves. Generally these insects are widespread and can be discovered upon close

Chiggers are actually mites. They wait for any animal or person to pass by to allow them to spread to different areas.

examination of grass blades that have turned yellow in distinct circular patches. They particularly enjoy St. Augustine grass, but Kentucky bluegrass and bent grass are also affected.

For chemical control use propoxur, isophenphos, diazinon, chlorpyrifos, or NPD.

Cinch bugs suck juice directly from grass leaves. Generally these insects are widespread and can be discovered by examining individual blades.

Crane Flies lay eggs that produce grubs which feed on grass blades. This causes patches of grass to disappear, usually from the edge of the lawn. Sometimes a brownish paste will cover an area with a large concentration. Crane fly grubs are brown-gray and about an inch long.

For chemical control use diazinon.

Cutworms are extremely difficult to spot, not only because they live and stay far down in the root system, but because the appearance of the damage they cause is similar to that of so many other diseases and ailments. Cutworms eat the tender roots of the plant and this causes dead brown spots to form in round and irregular patches. If a person were to spill gas or use too much fertilizer in an area, the effect would be the same as the damage done by cutworms.

For chemical control use acephate, carbaryl, diazinon, or chlorpyrifos.

Cutworms can be seen by removing sod from a small area. They are sometimes found curled up in round balls. The winged form is also shown.

Greenbugs suck juice from the grass blades and at the same time inject a poison into the plant. They cause rust-colored patches of grass that turn brown and die. These patches start under trees and spread to sunnier sections of lawn. Greenbugs are very small aphids that like many grasses but seem to prefer Kentucky bluegrass.

For chemical control use acephate.

Grubs feed by sucking juices from and eating the roots of grass plants. They can be difficult to diagnose because they live down in the sod. Also, there are hundreds of different kinds of grubs that will live in a lawn at different times of the year, in different stages of development. Indications are brown patches, irregularly shaped, and affected sections will roll back as if made of carpet.

For chemical control use trichlorfon, chlorpyrifos, diazinon, or isophenphos.

Mole Crickets eat grass roots and cause irregular streaks of brown and wilted grass. Dead and dying grass will pull up very easily. Tunnels can be

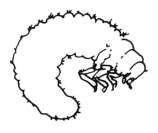

Grubs are the larvae stage of many different types of insects. They live in lawn-root systems.

easily seen if the ground is bare. Mole crickets are about two inches long and are brown or gray in color.

For chemical control use propoxur and diazinon.

Root-Feeding Nematodes feed on lawn roots and cause grass to grow slowly and to respond poorly to watering and fertilizing. Often the grass looks stunted and yellowed with dead and dying areas. Sometimes this problem is confused with fertilizer burn, soil deficiency, and poor aeration. The grass roots may be swollen, stunted, bushy, and dark in color or missing altogether.

There are many thousands of kinds of nematodes, but only a few damage lawns. Complete diagnosis will require the assistance of a competent nematologist. Likewise, for control, only a professional should complete any kind of necessary application.

Sod Webworms live in the grass root system, but they surface to devour leaves and stems with an insatiable hunger. Dead patches from one to two inches in diameter appear among otherwise healthy, normally growing grass. Many birds feeding regularly on the lawn can indicate a high concentration of this insect. Sod worms are not as easy to spot as cinch bugs, but they can be

Sod webworms live in the roots but devour leaves. They are difficult to see but can be found by searching a grass clod.

discovered by examining a few two-inch clods of grass taken from various portions of a suspect area of lawn.

For chemical control use carbaryl, chlorpyrifos, diazinon, acephate, isophenphos, propoxur, NPD, or trichlorfon.

INSECTICIDES

When it becomes necessary to use an insecticide as a pest control, be extremely careful to read *all* instructions on the label. Also, seek out and heed the advice of local professional gardeners or nursery staff.

Acephate is used for armyworms, greenbugs, and sod webworms.

Carbaryl has many forms, varieties, and uses. Manufacturers market it to control several insects including cutworms, cinch bugs, and sod webworms.

Chlorpyrifos is used on cinch bugs, sod webworms, and grubs.

Diazinon is used for many different insects but works best for long-term control of grubs. It comes in many forms and is made by many different manufacturers.

Isophenphos is used for cinch bugs, mole crickets, grubs, and sod webworms.

NPD is used for cinch bugs and sod webworms. It lasts for up to eight weeks.

Propoxur is used on cinch bugs, earwigs, and leafhoppers. It is often seen in insect baits.

Trichlorfon is used for grubs, sod webworms, and mole crickets.

Note: For forty years people have been using dursban to combat many of the worst lawn and tree pests. Hardly a property owner in the U.S. has not used dursban at least once, if not many times. But late in the year 2000, dursban was determined to be too dangerous to the eco-system for common use. It cannot be emphasized enough that chemical compounds currently available today may not be tomorrow. Cultural methods, on the other hand, are always being developed with better and better results.

CHAPTER
13

Organic Lawn Care

The internet has brought about an information revolution. With just a few words entered into the proper search engine, volumes of timely information can be retrieved for in-depth study. In my own intensive research into newer and ever-changing methods of lawn maintenance, I have found a powerful trend that, in my opinion, is of great benefit not only to our separate communities and even the nation, but to the entire world as well. This trend is toward the successful exclusive use of *organic* maintenance in all phases of gardening, property care, and lawn care.

Organic, here, refers to the use of naturally produced products, and naturally occurring methods of care and maintenance. There is much argument over which methods and products are organic and which are not. Generally, though, if you are using synthetic chemicals to get a result, you are not utilizing organic methods. I have met many people who refuse to consider the benefits of organic methods and products. Conversations with these people make me feel sad and worried. These individuals, who believe in indiscriminate use of herbicides, pesticides, and fungicides, are unaware of just how large the world's population has become. They do not realize how many millions of gallons of destabilizing chemicals are poured into our soil layers and water tables each year.

When a property owner sprays a weed patch, he or she generally justifies the use in two ways. First, the product wouldn't be sold on the market if it were dangerous to use; so it must be safe. And second, they tell themselves, "I'm using such a small amount; it can't possibly do any harm." They either do not realize, or do not *want* to recognize, that millions of people every day are using the same rationalization to do the same thing. These small amounts of toxic chemicals added together represent a phenomenally dangerous sum. It translates into millions of gallons of toxic chemicals polluting our world every year. When the statistics of chemical use are studied, the facts are quite sobering. Farmers who use chemical controls experience a high incidence of deadly diseases including leukemia and cancers of the liver, prostate, stomach, skin, brain, and lip.

As for the assumption that a chemical would not be sold on the market if it were dangerous, just look at the herbicide atrazine, which has been banned in many countries (including Germany, Italy, Sweden, Norway, and the Netherlands) but is still widely used in the United States. This chemical damages the liver, heart and kidneys. In addition, atrazine, like many synthetic farm chemicals, mimics estrogen and has been linked to reproductive disorders including decreased sperm count and sterility in men and an increased incidence of breast cancer in women. Studies are underway to determine the relation of atrazine to birth defects as well. There is more than enough hard and soft evidence to demonstrate the necessity of changing to organic and cultural methods instead of using chemicals. Following are some proven effective examples of organic lawn care methods.

FERTILIZERS

In the case of fertilizing, there are many products and procedures that are regarded as organic and natural.

1. Simply cut your lawn without a bag and leave the clippings to feed the lawn. Or better yet, use an up-to-date mulching mower to pulverize the grass. This process can supply your lawn with up to 90 percent of the nitrogen it needs. The only caveats to this practice are that the grass must be cut as fine as possible and not be left in clumps.

2. Use ground manure in light and regular amounts, since just leaving the clippings does not provide enough nutrients to keep a lawn in peak condition. Regular use of manure will yield a lush, green lawn.

3. If manure is not available, then use minimally processed sewage, another natural form of fertilizer. It is good to use sewage, in part because there is little other use for it, and there is a lot of it produced naturally on a regular basis! Often this is called *Urea*. One of the best features of urea is that you can dump the stuff on thick and still not burn your lawn.

Most synthetic fertilizers are made up of the exact same elements as natural fertilizers like manure. Synthetic fertilizers are many times more concentrated than organic fertilizers, but they do not have as many micronutrients. This means that you must use far more of a natural fertilizer to get the same results you would achieve with smaller amounts of synthetic fertilizer.

Do not let the word *synthetic* fool you. Many individuals define the word as something that is unnatural and therefore undesirable. In the case of fertilizer this is not quite true. *Synthetic* just means concentrated, not that it is not produced by an organism. While potassium is extracted naturally from plant matter in the process of an animal's digestion (manure), it can also be synthetically extracted from plant matter by a machine through more efficient but mechanical means. However, the use you put it to is, organically speaking, still the same.

The truth is, synthetic fertilizer ceases to be considered *organic* and *natural* only when chemical additives such as pesticides and herbicides are added to it. It is these unnatural chemicals that, when overused, have been blamed for the death of animals and plants and the contamination of food and water. But it must be remembered that this has only been proven to be the case when large amounts are used.

PESTICIDES

Unfortunately, the most effective pesticides are still inorganic. If an organic method is desired, however, there are viable options.

1. In cases where a certain pest is known to exist, choose and plant a cultivated variety of grass that might be resistant to or unaffected by the particular pest. These pest resistant varieties become more numerous every year.

2. In recent years certain diseases such as milky spore disease have been studied, developed, and used to combat pests. The above-mentioned disease, for example, attacks Japanese beetles, but it can take five years to spread far enough to be effective. At the current rate of development it could be many years before this means of ridding an average lawn of a troublesome pest is developed well enough to be of more than limited use. But with research into organic methods becoming more of a priority, methods like this could possibly be made useful in the near future.

3. Another option is to introduce a pest into a lawn that is harmless to grass but will devour harmful lawn pests. Because there are always unforeseen ramifications when an outside predator is brought in to a new eco-system, this method has not yet seen active commercial or home use. It may, however, be possible in the future.

4. Make sure that your thatch base is not more than a half inch or so deep. Many pests find a deep thatch base to be a good place to set up a new colony or two. Other pests require the thatch base to be deep enough or they cannot produce offspring.

5. Be certain that your watering program is sufficient to keep your lawn growing at peak efficiency. Lawn pests generally do not enjoy a damp humus soil because they themselves are subject to contracting parasites and disease if their environment is not dry and warm for extended periods of time.

6. Even when a lush and healthy lawn does have a parasite, it can go quite unnoticed. Adherence to regular maintenance schedules, along with good fertilization techniques, will usually keep a lawn healthy enough to fight off pests.

At the present time, most biological methods of pest control seem to have the same drawbacks. They only attack one type of pest and take up to several years to work. This will likely change in the near future if the current trend towards organic care continues. The best way to stay apprised of any possible updates is to maintain contact with a local nursery person and to do some occasional serious research on the internet.

HERBICIDES

All chemical herbicides are considered inorganic. Some kill seeds while others attack roots. Some chemicals kill only a weed's leafy structures, leaving the main stem, deprived of nourishment, to die. But regardless of the point of attack the potentially disastrous cumulative effects on the water table and food supply are still the same. The organic methods of weed control are simple to learn and put into practice.

1. *Pull weeds out by hand.* This takes time and effort, and only two-thirds of the pulled weeds are permanently removed. The reason for this is that it is just about impossible to remove the entire root of a weed from the intertwined root system of a growing lawn. A good example is the dandelion, which sends down a root sometimes as deep as two feet. And if upon removal only two inches is left, the weed will return.

2. *Keep a lawn thatched and well aerated for good drainage.* When a lawn is aerated well, the grass grows thicker with the root system more closely entwined. This makes it harder for weed seeds to germinate and grow.

3. *Institute a good fertilizing and watering program.* A healthy lawn is the best deterrent against weeds. When a lawn is fed well and correctly so that it grows thick and green, weeds cannot find a place to take root. When thatch has been kept to a minimum, weed seeds and fungus will find no place to shelter and grow.

4. *Plant cultivated varieties of grass that are resistant to weeds common to your area.* Every month new cultivated varieties of grass are created for different climates. These will thrive well enough to keep weeds in check. Though they can be difficult to find, these cultivated varieties are available if you are willing to look hard enough.

5. *A good mowing schedule will keep many weeds from flourishing.* When stems and leaves are chopped on a regular basis, some weeds will die from the sustained damage. Others, though they survive, are cut down to an almost unnoticeably low profile. If you have a sufficient maintenance program throughout the year to keep your lawn thick and healthy, during the winter, many annual weeds will die out and not return in the spring because there is no room for germination.

Unfortunately, the organic battle against weeds is an endless one. Weed seeds permeate soils by the millions and they are continually reshuffled and moved around by animals, people, and machines. But remember that even with the use of an effective herbicide, this battle will go on. A healthy lawn, however, gives you a tremendous advantage.

LAWN MOWING

Most methods of organically mowing a lawn are not very feasible or efficient. One way is to use a grass-eating herbivore to devour the blades as they grow. Sheep will do the job and so will horses! But they are not too meticulous about keeping the grass even, and in most urban areas there are zoning laws that would keep them out even if they did an impeccable job!

Why would someone want a method of organic lawn mowing? Because with the number of lawns created around the world and the amount of pollution contributed by mowing machines (both noise and airborne), many people are searching for a better, less harmful way of cutting their grass. Here are two plausible, reasonably ecologically sound lawn-mowing methods.

1. *Instead of using a gas-powered mower, use an electric mower.* They are quiet, they do not pollute directly and they are very efficient in terms of start-

ing, running, and wear ratios. The only drawback is the necessity of ob-
taining and using an extension power cord that is long enough to reach
every corner of the area to be mowed. There are now battery-operated
mowers which are charged overnight and are capable of mowing an average size lawn within the span of a single charge.

2. *Do not let your lawn grow fast.* In the last five years, slow growing varieties
of grass have been developed that need cutting only half as many times
per season as traditional lawn varieties. Some of these varieties require
less water and fertilizer as well.

As people grow more concerned about the environment, and laws are
passed to protect the planet from harmful substances, new methods for old
procedures are developed. In one large city in California, a bill has been
proposed that would require all residents within city limits to use electric
mowers.

In other states where drought has continued for three years or more, fines
of up to one thousand dollars have been issued to citizens who insisted on
watering their lawns in violation of emergency orders. In many of these
drought-stricken areas people are turning to new methods of landscaping
without lawns, using plants that require much less water and maintenance.
These designs are called *xeriscapes.*

A xeriscape is a landscape that requires little or no watering and little or no
weeding. This approach also eliminates the need for weed killers, pesticides,
and fertilizers. But these dry and rocky styles of design are little comfort to
those of us who still love a soft, green lawn. Xeriscapes also do not help create
watersheds or assist in the process of oxygen production.

With the great move toward organic and cultural methods in all phases of
gardening it might be possible to cut the use of chemicals down to a fraction
of their total use at present. This would mean wonderfully luxuriant lawns,
with virtually no damage to our ecosystem. Certainly, this is a goal that
should please even the most ardent user of pesticides, herbicides, and fungicides.

CHAPTER
14

Repairing Damaged Lawns

Whether by insect, weather, disease, or neglect, lawns are often damaged right down to bare dirt. There are many ways to repair damage; which approach to use depends on how the area was damaged in the first place. The following information suggests methods of repair for a broad base of general damage.

SYNTHETIC CHEMICAL AND FERTILIZER SPILLS

The grass here will turn yellow and die. There will be no sign of a root system when the soil is checked. In this case the soil may be infected for a period from three months to five years or even more depending on what has been spilled.

All soil to a depth of five inches must be removed from the dead area. Replace the soil with new high-grade dirt. Either sod or seeds can be planted. If the replacement is to be done during the hot summer season, then sod is best. Be sure to match the grass variety with that of the existing lawn. If this is not done, the replaced areas will be of different texture and color. The difference will be noticeable for a while, but eventually the intermingling of root systems can blend the two varieties.

BARE AREAS CAUSED BY HEAVY TRAFFIC

In this instance the soil will be compacted and hard. Neither seed or sod can get a hold. If reseeding is the chosen method of replacement the bare areas must be aerated extensively. A good raking with a metal-toothed tool is required. This should be done to a depth of at least a third of an inch. A good high-traffic variety of lawn seed should be used.

If sod rather than seed will be used for replacement, the soil must be removed down to a half inch in depth in order for the soil level to remain constant with the level of the surrounding areas. Extensive aeration should be performed after the soil is removed. The sod should be of a hardy variety, and it should not be rolled after placement as this will compact the soil. Regular aeration is necessary in all high-traffic areas.

DAMAGE CAUSED BY INSECTS

Be certain that the pest is eradicated. It is best to institute good fertilizing and watering procedures to strengthen pest-weakened grass. In most cases it is better to overseed than to dig up any remaining lawn and plant sod. When overseeding, if possible, mix in a cultivated variety that is resistant to the particular pest that has damaged the lawn.

BARE SOIL LEFT BY REMOVAL OF WEED PATCHES

It is possible to use seed or sod in this situation. No real soil removal or preparation is needed other than that which is standard. A hardier grass variety might be desirable—one that will grow thick enough to prevent weeds from gaining a hold.

GRASS DEAD FROM NEGLECT

There are cases of lawns, not having been watered for more than two years and having a complete brown and dead appearance, that, after aeration and continued deep watering, have recovered to become strong and viable. Grass has been around for thousands of years longer than we have had sprinkler systems, and it has adapted to survive drought cycles that sometimes lasted decades. Before spending the time and money to completely replace a lawn, be sure all avenues of watering, fertilizing, and maintenance have been explored.

WORN-OUT SOIL

Sometimes a lawn is planted in an area with extremely poor soil. Usually the soil will consist of too much gravel or too much sand with little or no loam and humus. When the grass is grown for many years with few or no fertilizer applications and the cut grass blades are always bagged and thrown away, the result is a plot of grass that is thin and weak. If overseeded, none of the seeds will germinate. Fertilizer helps to green the lawn, but it gets no thicker.

In this case the only real alternative is to cover up the old lawn with at least five inches of grade A topsoil. Five inches is the minimum—the more the better.

Do not worry about removing any portion of the old lawn. Just be certain it is covered completely with new soil. Then a layer of fertilizer and either sod or seed can be planted.

TREES

If a tree is planted close to a lawn border and too little water is provided, the tree will maintain feeder roots along the soil surface. The only way to avoid this is to be certain that all trees in a yard receive long and deep watering so that their feeder roots seek moisture well below the surface.

Once the damage has been done, however, a lawn will have veins of dead grass running throughout like a map tracing. This is because the tree depletes the grass of all available water and nutrients. The only way to remedy this is to remove the tree and start over. The roots themselves must also be removed and this is often a terrible job. Some neglected homes have needed a bull-

Remove grass that girdles a tree, whenever possible. Either keep this ground bare or plant flowers. This keeps the tree trunk from being damaged, and it gets rid of the problem of unhealthy grass growing in the shade and water deprived areas beneath a tree.

dozing of the top two feet of soil to get rid of the problem wood. When the removal is complete, new soil must be brought in and seed or sod can be used.

DAMAGE CAUSED BY DISEASE INFESTATION

A lawn damaged by disease is usually an indication of other problems as well. It might be necessary to replace soil or to upgrade the sprinkler system. It is important to discern the cause and make adjustments. When the cause of the infestation has been discovered and treated, plant a new variety of grass that is resistant to the previously manifested disease.

Remember:

A lawn that is healthy and strong will resist damage. And when damaged, a healthy lawn will recover quickly and easily. Devoting the time to watering and fertilizing means less time spent on lawn repairs.

Keep in mind that overseeding—scattering a different variety or grass seed throughout an existing lawn surface—is a great way to change the appearance of an ailing lawn. You do not have to worry about eradicating the old lawn before planting the new one. And though you might be planting an entirely different texture of lawn, as long as the seed is planted and scattered uniformly, the grass will blend perfectly in appearance.

CHAPTER
15

Lawn Care Tips from the Professionals

After seventeen years of working on thousands of different lawns, I've formulated a few helpful and quick tips for different aspects of lawn care that everyone can use.

LAWN MOWER MAINTENANCE

1. To extend the life of a lawn mower, be certain to completely drain and change the oil at least once a year. If possible, change it twice a year. Professionals change the oil twice a month.

2. After every mowing, hose down the undercarriage of the mower. Moist grass sticks to the bottom of a mower. If it is left to dry, the protective paint will be eaten off, and the undercarriage will rust away. Also, grass stuck to the undercarriage makes for less efficient cutting. Though this is an important issue with all mowers, it is critical for mulching mowers.

3. Once a year, fill the mower tank with a 50-to-1 mixture of gasoline and two-cycle oil. This will lubricate the engine and keep it running free and well. If you do this more than once a year, however, it will foul up the spark plugs and valves.

4. Do not leave grass in the grass catcher. This will quickly rot the material. Hang a catcher up to dry if possible.

5. Keep the bolts on your mower handle tight. If they get any play in them, stress fractures will result and the handle will break.

LAWN CUTTING

1. Use a good self-propelled model—these take the drudgery out of dull weekly mowing. They are more expensive, but in the long run a self-propelled mower makes an owner wonder why he or she ever used anything else.

2. Keep your lawn mower blade sharp. With a sharp blade a lawn mower will cut faster and more easily. Mowers do not become bogged down with even wet grass when a blade is sharp. Also, a lot of lawn damage can be avoided with a sharp blade. When grass blades are torn instead of cut, parasites, fungus, and disease get into the grass much more easily.

   To sharpen a blade, remove the blade from your machine and run the edge along an electric grinder wheel or have it done by a professional. The sharper, the better!

3. Cut a lawn as long as possible. Longer grass survives the trauma of cutting better and uses much less water. Longer grass blades have a greater surface area to absorb sunlight. When more sunlight is absorbed, more energy can be taken in to feed the plant. When the plant is fed more energy it naturally becomes stronger, more healthy, and luxuriant.

4. Mow a lawn only when the grass blades are dry. This is easier on your mower and the cutting will look better. Dry grass cuts with a much cleaner edge. Cutting a lawn in the morning when dew is still present is not a good idea. Since cutting a lawn in the late morning or early afternoon subjects one to the hottest sun of the day, evening is the best time to mow.

5. If a gas lawn mower is being used, be sure to fill the gas tank on a non-grass surface such as a garage floor or a driveway. Do this each and every time before you mow. This is necessary for two reasons. First, if a gas tank is full, a mower will run better with less trouble. Second, if you run out of gas in the middle of a lawn, the temptation is to run and get the gas can and bring it to the mower rather than push the heavy mower over to the gas can and then back to the cutting area. When a can is brought to a mower and used to fill a tank while the mower is sitting on a grass surface, drops will *always* spill and cause dead spots. This is a common occurrence, but it can be avoided easily. If a company is doing your lawn for you, be certain they too are filling their tanks on the driveway or road.

6. Use a mulcher mower whenever possible. This will help a lawn enormously, and it will save work for the person doing the job because they will not have to keep emptying the bag!

7. Buy a pair of golf shoes and wear them when you cut the lawn. This will help to aerate the lawn. Though not nearly as good as an aeration machine, it can be quite helpful.

8. When using a weed-trimming machine, always trim in the direction that the weed eater turns. If a weed eater cuts in a clockwise motion, you should trim your lawn in a clockwise direction. This lifts the blades to be cut right into the cutting path. To trim in the opposite direction that the machine turns will bend the grass blades away and they will not be trimmed well at all. When you are trimming the edge of a flower bed that's inside a lawn, however, trim counter to the spin. This will lift the blades of grass right up out of the bed and into the cutting path. Trimming in this direction will also flick the trimmed blades out into the lawn rather than onto a sidewalk or driveway, where they would have to be swept up.

9. One particularly important point that all professionals learn sooner or later is to follow religiously all of the precautions posted on any mowing machine. There are enough absent toes and chopped fingers out there to make it abundantly clear where and where not to place parts of your body that you might be fond of. Most of the accidents I have seen have been to the foot and toes. It seems people just do not realize how easy it is when you walk up to a running mower to have your feet project into the underside of the carriage and be swiped by the cutting blade. Never relax your guard around a mower. ALWAYS act with care.

FERTILIZING

1. Whenever possible, use a fertilizer with a broad range of nutrients. To use a straight mix of potassium or nitrogen or some other element is only a good idea when a soil analysis has proved the lawn deficient in that specific nutrient. Since a soil analysis is not always easy to obtain, a broad-range fertilizer has a good chance of providing what is missing. My favorite mixture is a 16–16–16.

2. Always fertilize as soon as possible after aerating. When fertilizer is applied while the aeration holes are fresh and still large, the fertilizer will wash into the holes and remain available for your lawn to feed off of for a longer period of time.

3. Apply small amounts of fertilizer on a regular basis rather than large amounts once in a while. This provides a lawn with a regular and easily used source of nutrients that will keep grass green and thick.

WATERING

1. A point that I have learned through years of experience in arid western climates is that many apparent ailments and dead spots of grass are the result of poor watering and drainage. Before any other remedies are experimented with, providing proper watering should be explored.

2. Water for long periods of time spaced farther apart rather than short periods of time once, twice, or even three times a day. This encourages deep rooting for greener lawns and better growth. The only exception to this rule is when you have a deep base of sandy soil that drains too quickly, or if you are establishing a new lawn.

3. Do not water during the day if at all possible. Far too much moisture will evaporate as the water is falling and after the water is turned off. Watering during the evening or night allows *all* of the water to reach the soil and then sink in deeply before the evaporative heat of day comes again. In some humid climates it is best to water only in the morning because watering at night in a humid climate allows water to sit too long, allowing fungi to get a hold in your lawn.

MISCELLANEOUS

1. When possible, remove grass completely from around any trees that are growing inside a grassy area. Instead, create a flowerbed or plant small shrubs. This will save a tree from dying because of damage done to the trunk by lawn-mowing machines and edgers as they bump against the bark. Also, grass generally does not grow well around the base of a large tree. A good garden around the tree looks better than ailing grass clumps.

2. Do not attempt to grow grass under pine trees. Pine needles that drop on a lawn secrete a resin-like substance that inhibits the growth of grasses. It has been suggested that pine tree roots also secrete this substance. If possible, cut off any branches of a pine tree that are within six feet of the ground. Then, create an attractive surface such as a flowerbed or ground cover area around the tree. Ivy grows well under pine trees. Also, keep pine needles from accumulating on the lawn surface.

3. Never let leaves accumulate on a lawn in a pile. If left too long, these piles will destroy a lawn.

4. Overseed a lawn every other year. This introduces newer and stronger cultivated varieties and keeps a lawn young and healthy. Spread seed over an existing lawn in medium quantities, then water for up to an hour to settle the seeds. This process is most effective if a lawn is aerated before the seed is spread. The aeration holes provide excellent homes for new seed.

CHAPTER
16

Lawn Care
State by State

Because weather and seasons differ from area to area, it is important to grow a lawn according to the natural conditions of your area. The same strain of Kentucky bluegrass that thrives in one area with continued watering may drown in another climate with only limited watering due to the differences in rainfall and humidity.

Following is a summary of conditions and growing requirements for each state.

Alabama

Much of Alabama has a 200-day or longer growing season. Central Alabama's season may last as long as 240 days. The climate in much of southern Alabama is influenced by the Gulf of Mexico; in some areas the growing season is 265 days.

Most of the soil is a variety of loam containing sandy, stony, or silty clay. A soil additive that is often needed is lime.

In the southern areas, heavy frost can be unpredictable because of the flow of cold air into lowlands and valleys. This obviously shortens the growing season.

North of Goodwater and Panda some cool season grasses such as Kentucky bluegrass and tall fescue can be grown with good results. The higher the elevation, the better the results. South of Jackson, Frisco City, and Ozark warm season grasses are mostly grown. Good varieties are centipede grass and Bermuda grass.

Alaska

In average Alaskan soils, organic matter such as dead plants, leaves, or dead grasses should be added to create the humus that is often absent. In swampy areas it is best simply to bring in new soil that will provide better drainage. Inland, the soil is usually low in potassium, nitrogen, and phosphorus. To compensate for this problem, a broad-range fertilizer should be added before sodding or seeding. It is often necessary to add lime.

Grass varieties that do well are Kentucky bluegrass and red fescue. Some of the cultivated varieties of Kentucky bluegrass, such as Nugget and Park, do well against the hard winter. Diseases such as snow mold are not uncommon, so disease-resistant cultivated varieties of red fescue such as Aurora and Reliant might be best. In areas with steep slopes it is a good idea to use a perennial ryegrass because it will grow quickly and hardily during the growing season. Some damage might occur, though, during the hard winter.

Arizona

Soil in Arizona is usually alkaline. The high alkalinity interferes with the ability of grass to absorb the necessary iron. In most of the state, fertilizers containing iron are necessary. Applications of gypsum will help.

Good grasses to plant are warm season grasses such as zoysia grass and Bermuda grass. Zoysia grass can grow in shade but has a slight susceptibility to pests. It is also a strain that needs de-thatching. Zoysia grass is slow to establish when seeded or sprigged. Bermuda grass is quite pest free and will look attractive. It can be planted from April to August but will look really brown during the winter season.

Arkansas

In the lowlands area the soil content is fertile and drains or holds water well as needed. Drought does not often trouble this area. The soil in the upland area is often severely eroded with low fertility content. Rain is distributed evenly throughout the year though slightly heavier in spring. Lime is often a needed addition to the soil.

The best and most common grass is Bermuda. Many people use improved cultivated varieties of Bermuda grass for better greening or heat and shade tolerance. Areas with 50 percent shade should utilize zoysia grass. This variety does not require as much mowing but forms a thick carpet covering. In some cases centipede grass is used (though it is slow to fill in) because it forms a very attractive lawn and can survive winter well.

California

The soil here is varied. Much of the state has alkaline soil and needs the input of organic matter to create viable humus. In soils that contain large amounts of sodium salts, gypsum is used to create a better balance. In much of north-western California lime has to be added to create good soil beds.

Because the climates vary from cold to hot, there are many varieties of grass that do well in different parts of the state. Kentucky bluegrass is grown widely but has restrictions in areas such as the Imperial Valley because of disease susceptibility. These restrictions also apply to areas in Ventura and San Diego. Perennial ryegrass is used in the northern and coastal regions, where winters are moderate. Ryegrass is popular, mixed with Kentucky bluegrass and some of the fine fescues, because it not only grows quickly but can improve disease resistance.

In hot areas cultivated tall fescues are used. This grass is very tolerant of heat and can look good if it is not mixed with other varieties. Bermuda grass also loves heat and can withstand long periods without water. This grass spreads well in the summer heat and will look green and hardy if it is fertilized well and mowed high. St. Augustine grass is sometimes used in California in areas with warm seasons but high shade. It does well only in these shade areas.

Colorado

Most of the soil in this state is alkaline without very much iron content. Iron-containing fertilizers must be mixed well with soils to grow thick grass. Some of the mountain areas are dry for much of the year and the good-grade soil is shallow. To keep a lawn growing, regular fertilizer applications are needed.

The most commonly used grass is Kentucky bluegrass, but because of a problem with leaf spot, it is better to use a cultivated variety such as Baron, Columbia, Midnight, or Sydsport, or even a blend of all four.

Thatch is common in many of the lawns because of the climate, but power raking will take care of this. One of the main causes of lawn problems in this state is inadequate watering. For best results a well-planned and regular watering program is essential.

Connecticut, Maine, Massachusetts, New Hampshire, Rhode Island, Vermont

The growing conditions in these states are quite similar. Both the soil and climate are relatively mild throughout the region. There is a large amount of rain, but the soil is usually shallow and not good at retaining water. Summer watering is essential; adopt a good watering program for best results. New soil is usually helpful. Lime is almost always a strong requirement.

The most widely grown grass is Kentucky bluegrass with sometimes a mixture of the fine fescues or perennial ryegrass.

Delaware, Maryland, Kentucky, New Jersey, West Virginia

These states are mentioned here together because of their similarities. The Appalachian Mountains and West Virginia have cool summers. Washington, D.C. and Maryland have hot summers. But throughout the region the rainfall is abundant. Many of the soils will be found to be adequate for ready planting. Others will be high in acid content and still others will be high in alkaline. Lime and gypsum are commonly used for these ailments. Testing to determine your soil content is often necessary.

Mixtures of Kentucky bluegrass, fine fescues, and perennial ryegrass are most useful in the cool summer areas. In hot summer areas it is best to use the tall fescues. A highly rated cultivated variety good for these areas is Kentucky 31. Bermuda grass is sometimes used in New Jersey, Maryland, and Delaware.

Florida

The climate is dominated by the ocean waters on three sides. There are several different soils. Along the coast there are marshes and sandy areas. Inland there are more fertile soils, especially those reclaimed from the swamps. Lime is often used.

There are many grasses that grow well in Florida—Bahia grass, Bermuda grass, centipede grass, St. Augustine grass, and zoysia grass. Bahia grass is better adapted to central Florida. Bermuda grass is used to make very attractive lawns in many areas. But centipede grass makes a good low-maintenance lawn in almost all areas (lowland or highland). St. Augustine grass, though mostly used in the shady areas, is the most popular grass in the state. But good watering, disease, and insect-control programs are essential to keep these lawns looking good. Overseeding all of these previously mentioned varieties is often done with perennial ryegrass and bent grass.

Georgia

More than half of the state has sandy soil, while the rest is mostly piedmont that is clay and clay loam. Almost all of the soil has a high acid content, but with lime and organic plant matter added it is capable of good growth with the grasses mentioned below.

The most popular grass is Bermuda grass, along with the cultivated varieties of Tifgreen, Tifdwarf, and Tiflawn. Where the soils are wet, however, a variety of grass called carpet grass is used. Centipede grass is used in wet soil but can be slow to start. For shade areas St. Augustine grass is used. In the mountains tall fescues are the most common.

Hawaii

Most soil in this state is sandy or volcanic and not very suitable for lawn grasses. To make an improvement it is necessary to add organic plant matter such as dead grass, manure, leaves, or compost.

A common variety here is Bermuda grass. It is hardy and can handle heavy traffic. Another grass that is used is Emerald zoysia grass. This variety is slow to establish but will become extremely thick in several years. St. Augustine grass is planted in Hawaii, but it is often known by other names. It will grow quite well in shaded areas.

Idaho

Idaho soil consists mostly of clay. Some areas contain rocks that must be removed before planting. It is best to make sure that as much organic material is worked into the soil as is possible.

Kentucky bluegrass is used most of the time but is often mixed with fine fescues to give it shade tolerance. If the cold of winter does not reach a certain area, perennial ryegrass is sometimes used. In the absence of artificial watering, the native American varieties of buffalo grass, blue grama, and wheatgrass can be used. These are strictly for non-ornamental coverage and require low maintenance.

There are many reported cases of powdery mildew and snow molds in Idaho; a grass resistant to these diseases is preferable.

Illinois

This state has three distinct climatic regions. The upper region (northern) has the coldest and longest winters with warm summers; the middle section of the state has cold to moderate winters with warm summers; and the southern section has mild winters with hot and humid summers. Over 65 percent of the state is prairie with a soil that is dark brown, deep, and fertile. In fact, most prairie soil was made and developed by long years of growing grass. Lime is often needed in the soil.

Kentucky bluegrass is the best and most often used grass, especially if a mix of red fescue or ryegrass is used as well.

Indiana

Half of this state is prairie with the typical deep fertile soil that characterizes prairie regions. The southern portion of the state has many hills, and though the soil is still quite fertile, it is shallower in many places. About 30 percent of the areas in the state will need lime added.

As in many other states, Kentucky bluegrass is the most popular grass variety except for some areas in the south. It can be beneficial in most areas to plant a mix of bluegrass with some of the fine fescues and ryegrass. For the southern areas it is best to plant varieties of Bermuda grass or zoysia grass.

Iowa

The climate in this state can be quite hot in the summer with hot, dry winds that can damage lawns that are not watered every day. The soil is fertile but often lacks lime.

Though Kentucky bluegrass and some of its cultivated varieties are used most frequently, tall fescues make tougher lawns more suited to high traffic.

Kansas

In the northwestern portion of this state the soil is acidic. The same is true for the southeastern portion. In western Kansas, where the great plains stretch out for vast distances, the soil is often windblown, and erosion is a great problem. Hardy grasses are needed to hold the soil in place.

Zoysia grass and Bermuda grass are used quite frequently throughout the state, but it is often more feasible to use the natural grasses, such as buffalo grass or blue grama. These natural grasses can be maintained on natural rainfall alone if necessary.

Louisiana

The greatest part of Louisiana is made up of level land with sandy but fertile soil. Much of the soil is acidic and regular applications of lime are necessary.

Centipede grass is the most popular variety because it will grow just about anywhere in the lower south, even in poor soil. But Bermuda grass will grow quite well in soils with moderate fertility. Sometimes St. Augustine grass is used for a well-kept and fertile area.

Michigan

Most soil in Michigan is highly acidic, but lime is not always directly applied because the water contains enough of it. Much of the soil is low in fertility, but if organic matter and regular fertilizer are added, the soil will produce a beautiful lawn.

The most widely grown grasses are cultivated varieties of Kentucky bluegrass and the fine fescues. These cultivars are Adelphi, Baron, Midnight, and Sydsport (Kentucky bluegrass cultivated varieties) and Aurora, Reliant, and Shadow (fine fescue cultivated varieties).

Minnesota

Soils in this state range from sandy loam to heavy clay. Add plant matter to these soils to increase fertility. Lime is not added more than once every five years or more.

Popular grasses are mixtures of Kentucky bluegrass and red fescue. Perennial ryegrass is also used in many areas, but it is best to plant a cultivated variety that is resistant to severe winters.

Mississippi

Both the plains and the river delta areas of this state are quite fertile. There are usually high levels of acid in the soil. Lime should be added on a regular basis in about 70 percent of the state.

Bermuda grass is the most popular choice. Zoysia grass, though it is slow to grow, is planted in some areas because it yields a more attractive and finer lawn. St. Augustine grass can be planted in the shady areas but will have only low winter tolerance.

Missouri

Much of this state is either lowland and slightly hilly, or prairie. The soils in all areas are quite fertile, but the prairie areas receive less rainfall and are less humid. Most areas are also quite acidic and lime must be added.

There are many varieties of grass that do well in this state, including Kentucky bluegrass, fine and tall fescues, and perennial ryegrass. Improved cultivated varieties of these strains work well also. Zoysia grass is used in a few areas where there is high heat and a long growing season.

Montana, Wyoming

These two states have very similar conditions. The soil usually lacks fertility, and a large amount of organic plant matter must be added to improve a growing area. Alkaline conditions are usually found instead of acid.

Kentucky bluegrass is the most popular grass but will grow even better if mixtures of fine fescues are also added. Fine fescues alone will form shade-resistant and drought-resistant lawns. Perennial ryegrass can be used, but it tolerates winter poorly and these states can get quite cold. In cases where supplemental water cannot be added, the native American continental grasses such as buffalo grass and blue grama grass are sometimes used, though not for ornamental purposes.

Nebraska

Soil in this state is usually sandy or sandy loam. Often the soil is shallow and needs improvement with organic matter. Lime is not generally added at any time. The winters are mild compared to other states but the summers are semiarid. Good watering programs are absolutely necessary.

Mixtures of Kentucky bluegrass and fine fescues comprise the most popular lawns. Perennial ryegrass is used in areas with the mildest winters. Tall fescues are used for hardy lawns in the dry areas but winter tolerance is not very good.

Nevada

This state's soil has high alkaline content and is low in fertility. Organic matter must be added to remedy this problem. Lack of water is a problem throughout much of the state.

Kentucky bluegrass with a fine fescue mixture is a common lawn blend. Tall fescues are planted in mixtures in some areas but for superior appearance they are best planted alone. In the southern dry areas, Bermuda grass is used almost exclusively for the finer lawns. Some Bermuda cultivated varieties are used for home ornamental gardens, but high maintenance is required.

New Mexico

The soil here is usually alkaline and low in fertility. Added organic mater is necessary. To wash salts from the soil it can be beneficial to flood a lawn area. Applications of gypsum will also help.

Bermuda grass is excellent for most locations where the heat is high and water may be available only in limited amounts. In areas where the weather gets cooler, Kentucky bluegrass is found. It is important to cut this grass as high as possible to help with heat resistance. In these same areas where the weather is cooler it is also possible to plant tall fescue blends.

New York

The climate in New York is mostly temperate with medium to high humidity. Summers can be hot and dry for short or long periods; so good watering programs are essential. Most of the soil is fertile and needs no organic plant matter added, but on occasion it is necessary to add lime.

Kentucky bluegrass mixtures are the most frequently grown varieties. Red fescue is often mixed with bluegrass to counteract the dry season problems. In the warmer areas of the state it is possible to plant zoysia grass for a beautiful lawn. Some improved cultivated varieties of these previously mentioned grasses will be more heat-, disease-, and pest-resistant for the New York region.

North Carolina

This state can be divided up into three regions: the Blue Ridge Mountains, the Coastal Plain, and the Piedmont. The soil is fertile in almost all of these areas but can be shallow in the mountains and Piedmont. The soil is quite acidic. Lime is always necessary.

In the western and mountain portions of the state the best grass to use is Kentucky bluegrass. In the lower elevations and flatter areas it is better to use Bermuda grass, tall fescues, or zoysia grass. In the warmer sections it is possible to use centipede grass or even St. Augustine grass if the area is close to the coast.

North Dakota, South Dakota

These two states are closely related in most conditions. In the eastern regions of the states can be found fertile, loamy soil. In the west the soil will range from extremely poor to excellent. In both the east and the west the fertile portions can be quite shallow and where this is the case, new soil must be brought in.

Most lawns are made up of mixtures of Kentucky bluegrass and fine fescues. If supplemental water is not available, the native American grasses such as buffalo grass and blue grama are able to withstand a hard and dry climate.

Ohio

The best soil in this state is in its relatively flat and even northwestern portion. The southeastern part of the state is mostly fertile, but because of the many hills, this fertile soil is usually shallow. In a few areas such as the north-central regions, the soil is often poor and stony. Soil will need to be brought in to grow grass in these sections.

The best grass for this area is undoubtedly Kentucky bluegrass. Some of the cultivated varieties such as Adelphi, Fylking and Sydsport are even better. In places of high shade some fine fescues can be used but are best mixed with Kentucky bluegrass.

Oklahoma

The western sections of this state are cool, dry, and flat, while the eastern portions are cool and moist with much more rain. Soil in the east is above average in fertility, while that in the west is only average. Both areas are good to excellent for growing grass. Lime is often required.

The most popular grass is Bermuda grass. A few cultivated varieties of Bermuda grass will do well also. In areas where supplemental water is not available or where ornamentation is not a factor, a native American grass such as buffalo grass will do well.

Oregon

In almost all of Oregon the soil is fertile with a lot of humus for good plant growth. On the west side of the cascade range the weather is mild, rainy, and humid. On the eastern side, the weather is colder and less humid, and the area receives much less rain.

Many different grasses will grow in Oregon. These include Kentucky bluegrass, perennial ryegrass, fine fescues, and sometimes creeping bent grass. In the western areas, improved perennial ryegrass is preferred, but it must be planted only where the winters are not severe. Cultivated varieties that are resistant to rust and red thread are recommended for most areas of the state.

Pennsylvania

The soils along the Allegheny Plateau are often stony and thin. The soils in areas similar to the Scranton area are mostly tough clay. In both types of areas a lawn will benefit from large amounts of organic matter added to the soil before the lawn is installed. Regular fertilization is needed in all areas and applications of lime are necessary in most.

Kentucky bluegrass is most often used. Some successful bluegrass cultivated varieties are Adelphi, Columbia, Glade, Midnight, and Victa. In the cooler areas, red fescue is sometimes used. This is the case most often where there is a lot of shade.

South Carolina

The climate in South Carolina is warmer than the climate in North Carolina. The soil of the Piedmont is relatively fertile but can be shallow in some places. The addition of good soil can remedy this. The soil of the coastal plains is fertile and deep in most areas and will grow grass quite well. Most of the soil is acidic and applications of lime will be necessary.

Where there are sandy hills or along most of the coastal plain, it is best to use Bahia grass. Bermuda grass is also used extensively and can be grown well in many areas. In the Piedmont regions, centipede grass is very useful and popular. On occasion zoysia grass is used, but only where the heat is not too severe.

Tennessee

In the eastern portion of the state there are many mountains that shelter broad fertile valleys. Though the soil in these regions is made up of sandstone, shale, and limestone, it is quite fertile and productive. There is a second area in Tennessee called the Central Basin, which is surrounded by ridges called the Highland Rim. This basin has fertile limestone soil and is most excellent for growing grasses.

Kentucky bluegrass is the most widely used variety. In many areas the use of zoysia and tall fescue is increasing. In areas of frequent drought it can be better to use Bermuda grass because of its ability to go without water for longer periods than other grass varieties.

Texas

Because of the size of the state there are many climates. In some areas in the east the rainfall is almost as abundant as anywhere in the country, and in some places in the west the rainfall is almost as scarce as in most deserts. Most of the soil throughout the state, however, is lacking in fertility and humus. Adding large amounts of organic matter can be extremely helpful for long-term lawn growth. Good fertilizer programs are necessary in most of the western portions of the state and lime is usually necessary in all areas.

The most often grown grasses are Bermuda grass and St. Augustine grass. Bermuda grass is the easiest to plant and care for, while St. Augustine is better at pest and disease resistance and can be quite attractive. A cultivated variety of zoysia grass called Emerald is used in some southern portions of the state because of its potential for thick green growth. But it will have little if any cold tolerance. In areas where water supplements cannot be used, buffalo grass will grow with only the natural rainfall, though it can be difficult to get started.

Utah

Almost all of the soil in Utah is low in humus and organic matter. Additions of plant matter are of considerable help before a lawn is planted. Most of the soil in the state is sandy and gravelly. In other areas there is hard-packed clay. In much of Utah there are high concentrations of alkali. Gypsum added to the soil will cure this problem. Another problem that will frequently occur is yellowing due to lack of nitrogen and iron. Nitrogen and ferrous fertilizers are a must. Summer drying is perhaps the worst lawn problem. In most areas sprinklers must be used every day.

Kentucky bluegrass is the most popular grass grown, but it does better when cut longer. Cultivated varieties that are resistant to high heat and dry air are more successful. For shaded areas, mixtures of fine fescues with Kentucky bluegrass should be used. Perennial ryegrass can be used for a quick-growing seeded lawn, but Utah winters are so harsh that only improved cultivated varieties such as Manhattan II are successful. In the extreme southern portion of the state near the city of St. George, some of the warm-season grasses such as Bermuda grass will do well.

Virginia

The soil in some parts of Virginia is acidic while that of others is alkaline. A soil analysis will confirm the pH, and either lime or gypsum can be added to counteract these problems. With care, most areas in this state will produce good lawns.

Tall fescue is planted most extensively in this state because it is a hardy strain. But other grasses can work well in the right areas. On the west side of the Blue Ridge Mountains and in many northern areas, Kentucky bluegrass, perennial ryegrass, or fine fescues should be planted. East of the Blue Ridge Mountains and in the southern areas Bermuda grass and zoysia grass should be planted. Cultivated varieties of Bermuda grass that grow well in the southern areas are Tufcote and Midiron.

Washington

Soils in this state are low in humus and plant matter. Any planted lawn will be helped by adding leaves, dead plants, and cut grasses as humus to the soil mix. Because of the acidity of the soil, lime must be added in most areas.

The best grasses to plant in the eastern regions of the state are mixtures of Kentucky bluegrass and fine fescues. In the western regions, perennial ryegrass will make a quick-growing and fine lawn. In the cooler and shaded areas of the western regions, bent grass is often grown for an attractive lawn.

Wisconsin

The winters in this state are very cold and harsh. Most of the soil throughout the state is acidic from the evergreen forest that covered it for hundreds of years. But if treated with lime and some fertilizers, the soil can be made dark and rich and will produce excellent lawns.

The best way to create a hardy lawn that will survive the rough winters is to plant a blend of three or more Kentucky bluegrass cultivated varieties. In dry, sandy, and shaded soils the use of fine fescue will produce an attractive lawn.

CHAPTER 17

Lawn Care Calendar

The timing of your lawn maintenance schedule is determined by the average mean temperature of your area. The growth of a lawn is influenced by many different components such as soil makeup, nutrient availability, and water, but the most prominent factor in lawn growth is heat.

Following is a broad-range lawn care calendar that divides the United States into three regions. These regions are determined not by placement on any map but by average yearly temperature, soil variations, and the length of the growing season. Conditions and timetables may vary for your particular area.

NORTH ZONE

North Dakota	Maryland	Connecticut
South Dakota	Delaware	Massachusetts
Nebraska	Indiana	Vermont
Kansas	Wisconsin	New Hampshire
Missouri	Iowa	Maine
Illinois	Minnesota	Pennsylvania
Kentucky	New Jersey	Ohio
West Virginia	New York	Michigan
Rhode Island		

SOUTH ZONE

Texas	Mississippi	North Carolina
Oklahoma	Louisiana	Florida
Arkansas	Alabama	Virginia
Tennessee	South Carolina	Georgia

WEST ZONE

Alaska	Arizona	Oregon
Hawaii	New Mexico	Washington
Utah	Wyoming	Colorado
California	Montana	
Nevada	Idaho	

NORTH ZONE

January to February

This is the time to treat any diseases, such as snow mold or gray mold, that have occurred in previous years. Do this during a winter thaw. Also apply pre-emergence weed controls at this time if you use this type of chemical. For cultural control, February is a good time to lay down an application of ammonium sulfate. This will jumpstart your lawn and encourage grass colonies to grow before weed seeds can germinate and get a hold.

March to April

This is a perfect time for planting either seed or sod. It is best to wait until the temperature reaches a steady 65 degrees Fahrenheit for laying sod, but it can still be placed anytime during the growing season. Seed can be sown during any thaw. The best growing time for seed is during the spring or fall when the temperature is between 65 and 80 degrees. This period is ideal for applications of gypsum, lime, or straight fertilizers.

Spring is a prime time for power raking. A lawn will recover quickly in an average temperature of 70 degrees with plenty of rainfall. Removing thatch will also help a lawn get better use out of a pre-emergence herbicide or fungicide.

This is a good time to aerate. Aeration will open up the soil to allow air, fertilizer, herbicides, fungicides, and even water to penetrate more thoroughly and deeply.

During these months, weeds such as crabgrass and dandelions will begin to sprout. Before the temperature reaches a five-day stretch of 65 degrees or more, there is still time to place some pre-emergence controls if you use chemicals. If the weeds are already growing, now is the best time to apply post-emergence controls such as 2,4-D, before the weather gets too hot (85 degrees or more).

Now is a good time to lay in applications of ironite and ammonium sulfate to give your lawn a jumpstart for the growing season, particularly if you do not use chemical controls or didn't perform this task during the winter months. Helping your lawn to grow as soon as warm weather appears will allow your grass to outgrow germinating weeds.

May

If heavy rains have fallen for a while and you utilize a program of heavy fertilizing once or twice a year, it is time to begin your regular fertilizing routine. If you have Bermuda grass or zoysia grass, it will be coming out of the dormant brown phase at this time. Amonium sulfate will speed up the greening process.

This is good weather for sprigging and plugging or sodding, especially in areas where Bermuda grass and zoysia grass are being planted.

This is a good time to overseed and add a grass mixture to your lawn that might make up for what your lawn is lacking—quick greening or disease resistance.

June

Fertilize any Bermuda grass or zoysia grass throughout the growing season. If you have adopted a weekly fertilizing program, apply each week after mowing.

If pre-emergence controls were not used for weeds, many will be growing at this time. It will be too hot to use most herbicides. A temperature of 85 degrees Fahrenheit is the outside limit for the efficacy of most chemicals. Carefully read all labels to determine current recommended usage.

During this month many insects will make their presence known. Brown dry patches will appear, and when the grass is lightly pulled on, it will pull easily from the ground or will roll back like carpet. Some insects will be observed at their work; others will need to be sought out by lifting a section of sod. Use appropriate chemical controls.

July to August

Cool season grasses will go dormant in the hot weather of these two months. Growing is slowed and greening becomes a problem. Continue watering and fertilizing for best results.

Warm season grasses such as Bermuda grass are growing fast at this time and will need nutrients (in the form of fertilizer) added in regular amounts.

August is a good time to prepare an area for a new lawn. You can take the time to add fertilizers and new soils and perform all of the necessary grading or leveling before the cooler growing season arrives.

This is the time when many adult beetles lay their eggs in the lawn. When they hatch, tiny white grubs will appear and feed on the grass blades. When cool weather arrives these grubs will disappear down to a depth of two feet or more to survive the winter. It is better to catch them now in the warm weather. Use appropriate chemical controls for best results.

Summer is also an excellent time for aeration. The holes provide better drainage for soils that are baked hard by the sun and allow fertilizers and oxygen to work more efficiently.

September

After the summer has passed, warm season grasses are still lush and green and cool season grasses are reviving with new life.

As the weather cools down below 80 degrees Fahrenheit it is possible once again to use herbicides to control weeds that may have experienced rampant growth. If cultural methods have failed, broad-leaved weeds can now be controlled this way.

This is the best time of the year for planting. The warm days and cool nights will encourage sods, sprigs, and seeds to grow fast and thick.

Power raking is done on established lawns during this time because grasses are able to recover more easily without the extremes in heat that summer brings.

Aerating is also recommended at this time. The holes will provide drainage for fall and winter moisture that can cause diseases and spores to grow.

September is also an excellent time to overseed both warm season grasses and cool season grasses. The seeds will grow well and fast.

October to November

For at least the first week and a half of October it is still possible to fertilize and plant. Fertilizer that has not been used and seeds that have not sprouted before snow falls will carry over to the next year. Fertilizer is important because it provides a lawn with a good strengthener before the hard winter season begins.

If snow mold was a problem during the spring, the disease organisms will still be present. Late October or early November is the best time to use a chemical to rid your grass of this problem.

Aeration for good drainage of fall and winter moisture is still recommended before the snow falls.

SOUTH ZONE

January to February

In the South, many areas will warm up quickly and pre-emergence controls will definitely be needed during these months.

In the warmest areas of the South, where some lawns stay green all year round, warm season grasses such as St. Augustine grass, Bahia grass, and Bermuda grass will benefit from an early application of fertilizer. This will make the dormant brown season shorter.

In states that are mild for most of the year it will be warm enough to bring grubs to the surface to feed on the grass. While at the surface, these grubs are vulnerable to chemical control if the conditions warrant such chemical use.

March to April

When the temperature of 70 degrees Fahrenheit is reached and sustained for more than five days, the growing season has officially started. Warm season grasses will begin to show new life through the dormant brown.

Fertilizer should be applied to several varieties of warm season grasses during March. Bermuda grass and St. Augustine grass are two examples. During April, carpet grass, centipede grass, and the cool season grasses should be fertilized.

It is good to set the mower low for the first cut in either March or April. This will clean out some of the old dead growth and allow warmth and sunlight to stimulate warm season grasses.

Although sodding can be done anytime during the warming season, these two months are an excellent time to lay down a new lawn. The warm days and cool nights before summer will encourage excellent growth.

There is still time to use a pre-emergence control for weeds before the temperature reaches a steady 65 degrees or higher. Check labels to be certain of correct use. If the temperature is higher than 65 degrees but still lower than 85 degrees, it is an excellent time to use post-emergence controls. Post-emergence controls work best just as the plants are sprouting.

In states where the spring weather is cool and moist for long periods, fungus and disease will grow and develop. Leaf spot and cottony blight are two examples. Appropriate chemical control is called for in extreme cases.

May

May is an almost perfect month for planting grass in the South. Warm season grasses can be planted later, but they might not have time to establish themselves before cool weather and the dormant season arrives.

It is important to fertilize all warm season grasses this month except carpet grass and centipede grass. If yellowing persists, fertilizers with iron may be needed. Any warm season grasses will need nitrogen also. This is a good month to apply either lime or gypsum according to need.

Power raking will be necessary for lawns that have accumulated one-half inch or more of thatch. This is especially true of Bermuda grass and St. Augustine grass.

Certain weeds will be in bloom at this time; dandelions are one example. Yet while spurge, oxalis, and others will not be blooming, they will be just as troublesome. Before the temperature reaches 85 degrees Fahrenheit or higher, it is important to use the chemical herbicides that are prescribed for the weeds of your lawn.

Aeration will (as always) be of great help in maintaining your lawn before hot weather arrives. Aeration will increase the water supply to the root system, allow fertilizer to reach feeder roots, and will allow needed air to circulate around the entire plant.

June

Cool season grasses will start to yellow and slow down as the weather gets hotter. Good watering will help with brown spots. Warm season grasses should be nearing perfection. But as with the cool season grasses, water is a main ingredient in keeping a lawn green as high heat sets in.

Weeds that have not been taken care of will really show during this month and the next. As lawns weaken from the heat, weeds are able to gain a better hold. Many of these weeds will need to be removed by hand, since the weather is too hot for most herbicides to be applied safely.

Both Bermuda grass and zoysia grass will require fertilizer during this month, since they will be growing profusely. Fertilizer need only be applied to cool season lawns that are on a weekly small-dosage program.

Sod webworms will become a problem this month. Moths hovering around a lawn at dusk to lay their eggs are the first symptom of this possible infestation. When the eggs have hatched, they will feed on grass blades at night and burrow in the roots during the day. Cinch bugs and armyworms will also appear at this time. Both of these pests can be seen during the daylight hours, though cinch bugs may require close examination for discovery.

July to August

During these hot months, water will be required in large amounts by all lawns. It is important to remember that deep watering will train a lawn to be green and flourish even during these high temperatures.

It is important to raise the cutting height of your mower for these two months to provide shade and evaporation protection. This will also keep a cool season grass from going dormant in the heat.

Keep fertilizing as needed, according to your program. Both Bermuda grass and zoysia grass will need applications.

If the weather in your area is hot, rainy, and humid, watch for diseases such as brown spot and gray leaf spot on St. Augustine grass.

September

This month is the best time of the year for planting any cool season grasses. The warm days and cool nights will accelerate growth.

As the weather cools below 85 degrees Fahrenheit, it is possible to use many post-emergence controls on weeds that have survived the spring campaign against them. It is also a good time to lay down some pre-emergence controls for certain annual grasses that are resistant to normal cultural and organic methods of removal.

At this time it is important to maintain a perfect fertilizing schedule. For the warm season grasses it is the last fertilizing opportunity of the year (except in the far South and when certain programs are in use) and will provide good growth in these fall days. For the cool season grasses, this is the time when fertilizer is stored in the plant system to help with winter survival. The better the fertilizer storage, the better the chances your lawn will come out of winter in good condition.

October to November

In the deep South there is still time to plant in October. Both months, however, are good for overseeding the warm season grasses with cool season grasses that will remain green and will hide the dormant brown color of the warm season grass.

The weather is perfect in most of the South for getting rid of broad-leaved weeds with chemical sprays. Many of these weeds are more easily attacked during this time of the year.

In the deep South it is time for the one last fertilizing that will build up strength in warm and cool season grasses for the winter months.

WEST ZONE

January to February

In areas of southern California and Arizona it is time to plant and fertilize. The mean temperature should be a sustained 65 degrees Fahrenheit.

In all areas it is time to get rid of crabgrass before it starts by using pre-emergence controls. It is necessary to have clear, dry weather in places such as Oregon, California, or Arizona before applying, and it is necessary to wait for a thaw before applying in places such as Utah, Idaho, or Colorado.

March to April

Now is one of the best times to plant cool season lawns. If sod, seed, or sprigs are planted, grass will have time to establish itself and gain a root system before hot weather arrives.

In Arizona and the southern parts of California the cool season grasses will be growing well at this time. In the other states the green will be beginning to show and the grass will get thicker. Warm season grasses will begin to come out of the brown dormant phase. Correct and regular applications of fertilizer will speed up the awakening process of both warm and cool season grasses. This month is also an excellent time for laying down gypsum or lime where needed.

Aeration before fertilizing will help a lawn absorb the nutrients much more efficiently and without waste. Aeration will also allow water and air to revive winter dormant grasses.

This month is a good time to power rake lawns that have more than a half inch of thatch because the cooler weather will allow a lawn to recover much faster. Removing excess thatch will allow water, sunlight, and oxygen to reach starving and choked root systems.

During the cool damp weather of spring, certain diseases such as leaf spot will appear. Fungicides will keep these diseases in check. When the hot weather arrives, many of these diseases will disappear.

May

There is still time (especially in the cooler north of this zone) to plant grass. For any warm season grasses that might need to be planted, this is the best time.

If a lot of rain is falling and washing nutrients from the lighter soils, it is a good idea to lay down an extra application of fertilizer. If weekly programs are being incorporated, be sure to follow the schedule regularly.

If a lawn has not yet been power raked, there is still time to have this job done and get the full benefit of the process.

Aerating for spring wakeup is still a good idea if it has not been done already.

If pre-emergence controls for weeds were not used earlier and your lawn is not strongly developed, the weeds will now begin to show. Dandelions and crabgrass are the easiest to see. If the weather has not yet reached a steady 85 degrees Fahrenheit, this is the best time to use post-emergence herbicides for large weed infestations.

June

Continue scheduled fertilizing. Cool season grasses store up nutrients that are applied at this time to use during the heat of summer.

Watering programs in all southern states and most northern states should be fully implemented by the middle of June. Deep watering should be utilized. As the daytime temperatures reach over 90 degrees Fahrenheit, brown patches of dry grass will begin to show and should be expected wherever insufficient moisture reaches the roots.

As the heat increases, most weeds are best removed by hand or by weekly mowing, since most chemicals will not work well in temperatures above 85 degrees. Certain annual grasses will begin to grow and then will turn brown and die in the heat of summer. In most of the northern or high-elevation areas where the weather is still cool enough, these can be dealt with by the proper limited use of chemicals. In other states it's best to wait until fall.

Cutworms will begin to appear in June. These worms love hot weather, and your grass will suffer accordingly. If you have had cutworms before, it is good to treat a lawn for them now. They are evidenced by brown and dying grass that will pull free with no attachment to any roots. Sod webworms will also become evident. The moths can be seen flying low over lawns and the worms themselves can be observed at night as they feed. Cutting and lifting up a square of sod can bring both pests to light. Use appropriate chemical controls, for they can spread very quickly, especially in the cooler Rocky Mountain areas.

July to August

In this hot weather, many cool season grasses will become almost dormant. Good watering and good fertilizing will help keep these lawns green. Most yellow and brown spots are the result of heat and insufficient moisture. Keep watering on an appropriate schedule.

Even if aeration has been done in the spring, many of the holes will be closed up and filled in by this time and another aeration job should be performed for maximum summer water use and greening.

Grubs will be plentiful during these two months. They will eat the roots of your lawn and the blades will pull free with no trouble. There are many different treatments for grubs. Many of these treatments can be used during even these hot summer months. Read labels for correct application. One point to remember is that no matter what chemical is applied, it is best to water thoroughly in order to help chemicals filter down more easily into the lawn.

September

As the hot days decrease and the warm days with cool nights take over, the best planting season of the year arrives. Cool season grasses will become established in plenty of time to survive the harsh winter months.

Fertilizer that is applied during this month will strengthen and restore lawns that have been depleted by the summer heat. Fertilizer schedules should be followed closely.

Power raking can be performed with excellent results during these cooler days if it is needed. This will provide more efficient use of fertilizer and sun for the remaining growing season.

Pre-emergence chemicals can be applied in later September to rid lawns of annual grasses that will seed next spring. If you use such additives, post-emergence controls can also be safely used for persistent broad-leaved weeds.

The last few weeks of September and the first few weeks of October are another excellent time to aerate, even if this procedure has already been done during the spring and summer. This will help fight molds, spore growth, and diseases that appear from fall and winter rains.

October

Good planting weather for cool season grasses will continue for several weeks in the warm southern areas.

As broad-leaved weeds continue to grow, it is still good enough weather for most of the month to use post-emergence controls.

This is a good time to overseed and add new mixtures of grass that have strengths which your present lawn might lack.

In the higher altitudes it is time to use fungicides for snow mold if it was a problem last year. The disease organisms will still be present and awaiting the right conditions to appear. Before any chemicals are used it is wise to check all labels and closely follow directions for use.

One last fertilizer application should be laid down. Much of this fertilizer application will be stored by the grass for use during the harsh winter months.

The last lawn mowing of the year should be short to keep the long blades of grass from compacting and creating a home for disease. This will help in spring cleanup next year.

CHAPTER
18

Troubleshooting

Trouble

BUMPY AND UNEVEN LAWN SURFACE

Possible Causes

- Worms coming to the surface.
- Tree roots growing near the surface.
- Presence of gophers and/or field gophers.

Possible Remedies

1. Worms rise to the surface and create mounds in an attempt to get oxygen into the soil. To alleviate this problem it is wise to aerate profusely and regularly.

2. To keep soils from compacting and locking out oxygen, use a drop spreader or broadcast spreader to lay down a layer of sand (never more than a quarter inch per application) over a lawn area to improve drainage. If a lawn is aerated first, the sand will trickle down in and fill up the holes for better distribution. This procedure may need to be repeated several times over a three year period to create the best drainage.

3. It is possible to use chemicals to get rid of worms. This is not always recommended because night crawlers are usually more beneficial than harmful.

4. Tree roots grow near a surface only when water is available on the surface for them to use. Watering programs set for long periods will encourage roots to seek water further down.

5. Remove all grass and cut out all problem roots. Then the grass can be replanted in clear soil. This is difficult and expensive but is sometimes

necessary. Water for long periods following this renovation so that existing trees will reach deep for water and the problem will not arise again.

6. Gophers and their smaller cousins, field gophers, love the soft soil of lawns. It is usually necessary to trap or poison these pests. Their holes must then be filled in well before a lawn surface will be even and able to support grass over the entire area. Long watering periods discourage these pests because they do not like their holes filled with water. They will seek drier, firmer ground.

Trouble

MOSS GROWING ON THE SURFACE OF THE SOIL

Possible Causes

- Too much shade covering this section of lawn.
- Poor water drainage.
- Improper fertilization.

Possible Remedies

1. If trees are causing shaded areas that block out the sun for most of the day, clear away low branches up to six or seven feet and dead branches anywhere on the tree. This will allow some light into a sunlight-starved lawn. As the lawn strengthens, it will fight off most mosses.

2. Aerate to allow proper drainage. As the surface water is drained off, the moss will not have enough moisture to survive.

3. Use ammonium sulfate to burn out moss. This will work quite well, but unless the problem that caused the moss to appear in the first place is remedied, it will return.

4. Plant a grass that is grows well in shade. A strong grass will not allow moss to grow.

Trouble

A LAWN GROWING THIN AND SPARSE

Possible Causes

- Poor fertilization.
- Poor soil content.

- Compacted soil.
- Improper watering procedures.
- Presence of grass diseases.

Possible Remedies

1. If the problem is fertilization, begin a regular fertilizing program. Be certain that iron and nitrogen are components of any fertilizer used.

2. If the soil content has too much clay, it is possible to aerate a lawn and then spread a light layer of sand that will fill in the holes, mix with the clay, and begin to help drainage. But if loam or clay needs to be added, it might be necessary to start over with a new lawn after first laying down a good base of soil. This is a drastic measure but necessary in some circumstances.

3. If a lawn is thin because water is not provided in appropriate amounts, a new watering procedure must be implemented. This new procedure should consist of a regular schedule and more uniform coverage. A good sprinkler system is the best method for turning this problem around.

4. If after studying symptoms closely a disease seems to be the cause, retain a professional to check for lawn diseases. If any diseases are found and confirmed, chemical procedures may be called for. Check with the professional before implementing.

Trouble

GRASS GROWING THIN IN AREAS SHADED BY TREES OR BUILDINGS

Possible Causes

- If grass is growing thin under trees it can be because tree roots are pulling all available water from the soil.
- The wrong variety of grass could be planted in the area.
- It is possible that not enough sunlight is present for any variety of grass to grow.

Possible Remedies

1. If tree roots are pulling the water from the soil, it is necessary to increase the amount of watering time under trees so that water will penetrate the

soil to a depth of three feet or more. This will encourage trees to seek deeper for water and to leave the surface alone. This should also leave enough water for both the tree and the lawn to flourish.

2. If the problem is that the wrong variety of grass has been planted in the shade of a building or tree, it will help to aerate the thin area and then overseed with a specific shade grass.

3. If the sunlight is too weak to grow any type of grass under a tree, try cutting back branches that are growing lower than six feet off of the ground. Thinning the tree growth by cutting back as many branches as possible will allow sufficient sunlight to penetrate and nourish the grass better.

4. If the building or tree is not allowing enough sunlight for any grass to grow, try cutting away what grass is left and putting in a border garden or flower bed that utilizes shade flowers or plants.

Trouble

GREAT AMOUNTS OF WEEDS GROWING

Possible Causes

- A field or uncultured plot of ground close by that is allowing many hundreds of times the average amount of weed seeds to continuously replant themselves.

- The lawn is being cut too short, allowing weed seeds to take an easy hold in the weakened grass.

- Poor watering procedures that create a weakened lawn where weeds easily take root.

- Poor fertilizing procedures that create a weakened lawn where weeds easily take root.

- Wrong variety of grass planted in the area and grows only poorly, allowing weeds to take hold.

Possible Remedies

1. If a field close by spreads a great amount of weeds into your lawn, it is best to use copious amounts of pre-emergence and post-emergence chemical controls. If some good herbicides are used on a regular basis, a soil will remain as weed-free as is possible under such circumstances.

2. If a lawn is being cut almost to the crown, allow the grass to grow longer before cutting. This will serve to strengthen a lawn and thus keep weeds

from growing well. This will also save a great deal on water loss due to evaporation.

3. A lawn that has hard-packed soil with no sign of water penetration usually suffers from incorrect watering. Aerate the soil well and institute a program of long periods of watering for deep penetration. This will strengthen the grass and allow it to fight back against weeds.

4. A lawn that is a constant yellow with thin blades is usually receiving deficient amounts of fertilizer or is deficient in soil content. If this is the case, utilize correct fertilizing procedures to strengthen a lawn against weed incursion. It might be necessary to establish a better layer of good soil. After this operation a new lawn will have to planted.

5. If no time is available for ascertaining the causes, retain a professional to analyze the problem and suggest the right chemical or necessary procedure.

Trouble

GRASS GROWING IN CLUMPS

Possible Causes

- Presence of crabgrass growing in the lawn.
- Poor soil content.
- Presence of toxic chemicals in the soil.
- Wrong variety of grass mixture.

Possible Remedies

1. If crabgrass is present, it will be necessary to either dig the offending clumps out, use post-emergence chemicals to kill the grasses, or wait until spring or fall to spray pre-emergence chemicals.

2. If the soil is nutrient-poor, it will need to be enriched with mulch, loam, and fertilizer in generous quantities. This can be done without removing the already present lawn as long as the new nutrients are thinly and evenly spread to a minimal extent over the entire lawn.

3. If the lawn grows in some clumps of thick and healthy grass and others that are thin and sick, it can be because chemicals that weaken grass are present in the lawn. The first answer to this problem is to spread a layer of nutrient soil over the whole lawn, wait until the grass grows up over this new soil, and then place down another layer. Repeat this procedure

until several inches of nutrient-rich soil cover the bad soil and the lawn is able to grow better. The second option is to totally remove all of the grass and lawn to a depth of 6 inches or more. Then fill in the space with grade A soil and replant the lawn with either sod, seed, or sprigs.

4. If the grass grows in clumps because of the presence of a fine grass mixed in with a coarse grass, the only options are to either overseed the entire lawn with the coarse strain or to remove the entire lawn and replant with the right blend of grass variety.

Trouble

PUDDLES OF WATER FORMING THROUGHOUT PORTIONS OF THE LAWN SURFACE

Possible Causes

- Clay soil creating poor drainage.
- Soil compaction.
- Uneven lawn surface.

Possible Remedies

1. If clay soil is present in a problematical quantity many difficulties will arise. The worst problem is that of the clay baking into a rocklike consistency when the heat of summer arrives. When clay soil bakes like this, grass roots cannot survive for any length of time. To alleviate this problem you must aerate extensively and then spread sand over the lawn in an even layer that will fill in the aeration holes and thus change the clay composition to a lighter and more drainable mixture.

2. Soil compaction is what happens when there is a lot of traffic on a lawn and the soil is pressed tightly down to the point where plant roots cannot breathe or get moisture through the light pressure surrounding them. Compaction will also occur when water in heavy torrents from frequent rains falls on a lawn, or even when sprinklers are used that spray water high and far to drop heavily on a lawn. Compaction will also occur when animals such as dogs make frequent use of a lawn, running and moving around on it.

   When compaction is a problem, the remedy is exactly the same as for clay. You must aerate at least three times a year and, whenever possible, spread in soils such as sand that are lighter in composition. It can also be wise to change the conditions that are causing the compaction—perhaps restrict the traffic or change to a different sprinkler type. These changes are options that are not always easy or possible.

3. Sometimes a lawn will have shallow depressions in the surface makeup; perhaps it was not rolled before the grass was planted or perhaps a deep below-the-surface problem has caused the ground to sink. Water will drain from the higher areas of the lawn and fill these depressions. Grass will have difficulty growing here and soil compaction will occur. These soil depressions should be filled with many thin layers of grade A soil, with several weeks in between each layering, to allow the grass to grow up over the new soil. This should continue until the surface is even throughout.

Trouble

A LAWN ROOT SYSTEM THAT ONLY GROWS TO A SHALLOW DEPTH

Possible Causes

- Light watering instead of heavy.
- Nutrient-poor soil.
- Hard, compacted soil.

Possible Remedies

1. Grass roots will reach only a shallow depth if water is applied in small amounts many different times rather than in large amounts less often. Small amounts of water only sink to shallow depths, and when water is to be found at a shallow depth, grass roots will stay there to take advantage of where the moisture is. Shallow root systems, however, dry up faster and burn up more easily in the hot summer sun.

   Water for long periods. This will cause the moisture needed by your lawn to be found in the depths, and with roots growing deeper, a lawn will stay green and thick even in harsh summer weather.

2. If nutrients are not present in soil, both roots and blades will have little to grow on. To get nutrients, institute a heavier, more regular fertilizer program. Add layers of nutrient-rich soil to the lawn whenever possible.

3. Hard, compacted soil causes a lawn to grub and strain for every tiny millimeter of penetration. The remedy for this is covered in the section of this chapter that deals with puddles of water forming on a lawn surface. Aerate and add lighter soil components.

Trouble

ENTIRE LAWN APPEARS YELLOW INSTEAD OF GREEN

Possible Causes

- Not enough nutrients in soil.
- Too much thatch.
  - Not enough moisture.
  - Not enough iron in the soil content.

Possible Remedies

1. Lack of a certain nutrient will cause a lawn to be yellow. When the soil makeup of a lawn is light and sandy, nutrients will wash out even with normal watering. In this case it is important to add fertilizer on a regular basis. The two main nutrients that when missing will cause a lawn to yellow are nitrogen and iron. Use a fertilizer that is heavy in these nutrients.

2. When dead grass in the form of thatch is thick and deep in a lawn, the general appearance is yellow instead of green. Power rake a lawn that has one-half inch or more of thatch. For the first week or so of a rake job the lawn will still be yellow because of the particles of dead grass that have been brought to the surface. Water extra for that week and the color will improve.

3. When a lawn utilizes cool season grasses and the summer heat reaches 94 degrees Fahrenheit and above, the appearance of the grasses can take on a yellowish hue. This is because cool season grasses such as Kentucky bluegrass will go into a semidormant phase to survive the heat. To avoid this dormant period even in the worst heat it is necessary to supply greater amounts of water and fertilizer to the grass so that it does not need to go dormant to survive.

Trouble

DIFFERENT-TEXTURED GRASSES

Possible Causes

- Wrong mixture of permanently planted grass colonies.
- Presence of new varieties of grass that have been brought in by animals, wind, or humans.

Possible Remedies

1. There are only two ways to correct the wrong blend of planted grass. The homeowner must select the hardiest (and this is also usually the coarsest) variety of grass in the present blend and then overseed the entire lawn with this variety. Or the homeowner can remove the entire lawn and start again with the right blend.

2. When a new variety is brought in by some accidental outside means, it will start to invade only a small area at first and then grow outward. This area will appear either finer than the rest of the lawn or coarser. When the invaded area is small it is easy to dig up the entire area of different grass (be sure there is not even one blade of grass left to carry on the strain) and then replace the spot with sod or seed. Sod is usually a quicker replacement, but the correct variety of grass must be matched or the problem will recur.

Trouble

DEAD OR DYING BROWN SPOTS

Possible Causes

- Presence of grass-toxic chemicals.
- Presence of lawn pests.
- Deposits of animal refuse.
- Too much fertilizer.
- Presence of lawn disease.

Possible Remedies

1. Retain professional help to analyze chemicals. If one has been spilled (gas is often spilled on lawns when filling mowing machines), it is necessary to remove the dead grass and the soil up to a depth of five inches or more. Then fill with new soil and replant the grass.

2. If pests are in the lawn, it will be possible to pull up the grass in a brown spot and have it come out easily with no roots attached. Sometimes the dead sod will roll back like a carpet. In this case it is necessary to ascertain the specific pest and to use a suitable chemical means to get rid of it.

3. If animal waste has been left on a lawn for even a short time before being removed it will overload the lawn with fertilizer nutrients. Brown spots

will occur. To prevent the brown spots and to help heal those that have already appeared, wash down the spot that the waste was on several different times with ten to fifteen minutes of medium-pressure water. Patiently wait for the grass to grow back. It usually will begin to grow back in three weeks.

4. When too much fertilizer has been laid down on a particular spot of lawn, dead brown patches will occur. These spots must be washed down with moderate pressure for half an hour at a time for several days. The grass will go back to green in anywhere from one month to one year, depending on the diligence of the flushing procedure and the amount of fertilizer spilled. Replanting can be done if desired. Soil replacement is not necessary for replanting as long as the area has been flushed several times.

5. If a disease is suspected, it is best to consult a professional. If a disease is confirmed, ask the same professional for advice on methods of cure. Many cures are listed in this book but a qualified nursery person will be versed in the latest advances in disease control. Follow this advice closely and if possible get a second opinion.

Index

Note: Page numbers in italics indicate illustrations

propamocarb, 88, 96
propoxur, 101, 103, 104
purslane, 80, *81*
PVC pipe, 25, 27–28

Q
quaking aspen, 82

R
railroad ties, 62
rainbird sprinkler heads, 29, *30*
red fescue, 6–7
red thread, 91
reel lawn mowers, 45–46, *46*
regulatory exclusion, 98
repairing damaged lawns, 111–14
  bare areas caused by heavy traffic,
    111–12
  chemical and fertilizer spills, 111
  diseases, 114
  important points, 114
  insect damage, 112
  neglected lawns, 112
  removal of weed patches, 112
  trees and, *113*, 113–14
  worn-out soil, 112–13
rhizomes, 4–5, *5*
Rhode Island, 124
  lawn care calendar, 136–39
riding mowers, 50, *50*
rock phosphate, 39
root-feeding nematodes, 103
roots, 4, *5*
  aeration and, 64
  shallow, 153
  watering and, 23
rotary-blade mowers:
  push type, *47*, 47–48
  self-propelled, *48*, 48–49

rotary sprinkler heads, 30, *32*
rough bluegrass, 9
rust, 91

S
St. Augustine grass, 7
sandy soil, 17
  watering and, 23, 24
sanitation and lawn pests, 99
scalping, 94–95
sedges, 77
seeding, 12–15
  coverage of, 12
  covering after, 13
  pattern for, 12, *14*
  as "survival of the fittest" method,
    15
  types of, 12
  watering after, 14
seed labels, *13*
shade grass, 3
sheath, 4, *5*
Siduron, 84
slime molds, 91
slopes:
  sodding, 15
  watering, 25
slow-release fertilizer, 40
sodding, 15
  soil preparation and, 19-20, *20*
  watering and, 15
sod webworms, *103*, 103–104
soil:
  bare, 112
  worn-out, 112–13
soil preparation, 16–21
  fertilizing, 18
  grading, 17
  important points, 21